'The bastard's a genius!' is what Fred Clifford (Robert's father) always said of his unusual first-born son. In Australian culture, the term 'bastard' has rich and varied meanings. There is the rarely used literal meaning (for the record, Robert Clifford was born in wedlock). There is the familiar pejorative meaning, as in 'he's a real bastard!' Then there is the subtler, near-affectionate usage we must assume Fred Clifford intended. Foreign readers need to know that in Australia, 'you old bastard!' is generally regarded as an expression of affection.

Cover photograph: Robert Clifford, aged just 40, holding the concept model of the first wave-piercing car-carrying fast ferry. Clifford the craftsman knew that this break-through concept was so important that the model had to be constructed not from cheap balsawood but from the extremely rare, honey-coloured Huon pine (*Lagarostrobis franklinii*)—one of the most ancient, slowest growing and beautiful of all tree species, found only in the southwestern corner of Tasmania.

The Bastard's a Genius

The Robert Clifford story

Alistair Mant

ALLEN&UNWIN

For Rosina and Lydia

First published in 2010

Allen & Unwin
83 Alexander Street
Crows Nest NSW 2065
Australia
Phone: (61 2) 8425 0100
Fax: (61 2) 9906 2218
Email: info@allenandunwin.com
Web: www.allenandunwin.com

Cataloguing-in-Publication details are available
from the National Library of Australia
www.librariesaustralia.nla.gov.au

ISBN 978 1 74114 366 9

Set in 12/16 pt Granjon by Bookhouse, Sydney
Printed and bound in Australia by Griffin Press

10 9 8 7 6 5 4 3 2 1

Mixed Sources

Product group from well-managed
forests, and other controlled sources
www.fsc.org Cert no. SGS-COC-005088
FSC © 1996 Forest Stewardship Council

The paper in this book is FSC certified.
FSC promotes environmentally responsible,
socially beneficial and economically viable
management of the world's forests.

Contents

Robert and me

This is the first time I have tried my hand at biography. That may, or may not, be an advantage. Robert Clifford, surveying his less-than-successful academic career, took solace in the thought: 'If I had received a regular education, I might now be building regular ships!' I'm not sure that a 'regular' biography will do in this case. It is easy enough to track the life of the subject from 1943 to 2010, but the really interesting and important aspects lie in the wake or the wave-patterns created by the hero as he ploughed through the centre of the story. In short, what makes Robert Clifford interesting is that he has made lots of things happen. So this is as much history as biography.

At any rate, biographers are meant to be dispassionate about their subjects' stories and to be uncompromising about what seems to be the truth—warts and all! Biographers are not allowed to fall in love with their subjects until they (the subjects) are long dead. Robert Clifford is very much alive and not short of opinions. So it is important to state that this is not an 'authorised' biography and I have had a completely free hand in pulling it together. I have talked to anybody I can think of in the Incat world and a great many outside. The list of those who refused to talk to me is a short one, and I think I can infer what they might have wished to say about Robert. My subject doesn't agree with everything in this book but nothing would induce him to interfere (apart from correcting technical errors).

The starting point was a chapter devoted to Robert Clifford which I included in my 1997 book *Intelligent Leadership* (Allen & Unwin). That chapter struck quite a few people as improbable but in fact it contained only two inaccuracies: the suggestion that Fred Clifford (Robert's father) was 'just a butcher'; and the intimation that Robert Clifford's secondary school had some hand in his emergence as an inventing and manufacturing genius. As I was preparing that book about leadership, a surprising number of people in the know told me: 'You'll have to include that bloke in Hobart—the shipbuilder!'

I tried for some months to get an audience with Robert and finally on 20 October 1995 received a gruff telephone summons from a hotel in west London: 'I'll give you half an hour!' Three hours later I left with the story in my head and my notebook and wrote the chapter that night. And that, apart from one technical correction, was how the chapter appeared in the book. The man himself was quite impressed at my ability to take it all in quickly and regurgitate it again comprehensibly. Each to his own skill; as I pointed out, I can't build ships. Now, nearly 15 years later, a lot of water has flowed under the metaphorical bridge, so the request from Allen & Unwin to undertake a biography was irresistible.

Not many people, I guess, would think of Robert and me as similar. I've lived so long in Europe, I now look more like a refined aesthete than I used to, while Robert looks as much like a beefy Viking pillager as ever. Yet, when it comes down to it, we share the formative experiences of wartime babyhood and the peculiarities of the post-war Australian class system. Those who argue that Australia is a class-free society weren't brought up in 1950s Hobart.

And we both loved our Meccano sets—an important bond when it comes to the world of real things in nature.

The big difference is that, for a variety of reasons (including having a journalist for a father), I became relatively bookish at an early age (it helped not being dyslexic). So my engagement with the excitement of big complex systems had to wait till I set out to work on the Snowy Mountains Scheme at the age of 19. In many ways, it was just an escape from the boredom of law school but, more than a diversion, it was a reconnection with physics, risk, enterprise, reality and all the other important matters that had preoccupied Robert Clifford in the first 20 years of his life. I was catching up. If you ask me now what is the best thing about writing a biography like this—it is getting to crawl all over these extraordinary ships as they take shape in the Hobart yard.

My admiration for Robert Clifford lies in the usefulness of his works—and in their sophistication. When I am not writing biography, I do my best to help various people in leadership roles to come to terms with (and manage) the realities of very complex systems. In the course of this work, I have been struck by the increasingly large proportion of the 'working population' engaged in essentially pointless employment activity. The world is in enough trouble already without so much waste of talent and ingenuity. It seems sometimes that half the population is being paid to create favourable impressions about big institutions of one kind or another. They come in the guise of spin-doctors, 'public affairs' consultants, financial advisers, advertising men, marketing whizz-kids, lobby-stalkers and a host of other taking-themselves-very-seriously-indeed forms. The other half of the working population seems to be engaged in trying to satisfy 'failure demand'—that is, responding to corporate failures of one kind or another, but with no hope of resolving problems or actually adding any value. Most of these poor souls work in vast factories known as 'call centres'. There must be a symbiotic relationship between the prevalence of failure and the demand for reassuring spin. None of it adds any real value to anything. It isn't real.

Contrast Robert Clifford and the dedicated workers of the Incat shipyard. The ships are real enough—and rather wonderful. Once they get to work they contribute substantially to communications in various parts of the world and they do so as efficiently as it is possible for any ship made today. And the development and improvement never ceases. It is the quintessential world of reality: if the ships don't sell, nobody gets paid; if the ships malfunction, the firm loses its hard-won reputation; if the bank loses the plot, the whole enterprise, and those who sail in her, is at risk of sinking.

So, in the end, Robert Clifford is a kind of alter-ego for me—at least in my capacity as writer/biographer. Books are solid objects and they do, occasionally, have some impact on events but I can't imagine anybody being awestruck by a book like this. But when I stroll or crawl around one of the Incat vessels, I am bowled over by the reality of it—in much the same way as I was captured by the immensity (and the comprehensibility) of the Snowy. So getting to grips with Incat and the genius behind it is a bit like reconnecting with the small boy with the Meccano set that I used to be. That's something to be grateful for.

Introduction

'Bob Clifford is a hero of mine. I actually sought him out because I wanted to find out how on earth he had learned to do what he has done. Everybody agrees it's impossible to manufacture sophisticated ships in Australia and sell them all over the world. These ships are as complex as a wide-bodied jet and most people say we can't build a sophisticated jet aircraft in Australia. How did he do it? I believe he is a genius and one of the most competent Australian inventors/manufacturers of all time.'

DICK SMITH

Technically, this is a biography of a remarkable entrepreneur. So it's a story about a man—Robert Clifford—who, from a more or less standing start, has succeeded in inventing an entirely new niche in the world market for ships, and in capturing about half of that market for Tasmania. But there is so much more to this story than an account of one man's mission to succeed in business.

So you can, if you wish, read the story as a kind of how-to-do-it primer for business success. As such, it may be of interest to business schools and their students—although the Clifford approach breaks just about every rule taught by the professors. In truth, Robert Clifford is in some ways a highly unsatisfactory businessman; his true *métier* turns out to be invention. In this he resembles other inventors-turned-businessmen like James Dyson and Thomas Edison. His company, Incat (International Catamarans), presents in these pages as a mere vehicle for his continuous and incremental invention.

Accordingly, there are numerous references in the text to business school orthodoxy—or to what the professors might 'teach' you via textbooks, case studies and 'subject' specialisations. Nowadays, Robert Clifford has a string of honorary degrees, but the truth is that, by his early twenties, he knew more about the dynamics of business operations than almost any business school professor—and he had no need of university to learn it.

So because Robert Clifford was regarded by most of his school-teachers as a complete dunce, this is also necessarily a story about the nature of intelligence and the incapacity of education systems to recognise and encourage any unconventional forms of 'brightness'. The story therefore poses questions for education policy and practice. Conceivably, if Robert Clifford had not been 'switched on' by certain chance events in his teens, his multimillion-dollar contribution to the Australian economy (and to global energy efficiency) might not have happened at all.

This theme leads into a reflection on the relationship of thinking to doing. Robert Clifford strikes most people as an archetypal doer—a man of action—but the really interesting thing about people who achieve great things is the cycle of experimentation (or play), making (or doing), and thought (or reflection) about what has just been done—and so on around the circuit. All artists understand this cyclical process and so do the great scientists. So it is no surprise that what links Clifford to his contemporaries Dick Smith and the Nobel Laureate Professor Sir Harry Kroto (see pp. 13–14) is the centrality of the humble Meccano set in infancy. As Sir Harry says: 'More than just a toy.'

Thus, it seems that making things makes you clever. A life spent entirely in the symbolic or 'academic' world renders you stupid in the end. (Discuss.) As it turns out, bankers play a central role in the drama of Clifford's business, so it is enlightening therefore to reflect on the mind-set of the modern banker—so removed from the cleverness of scientists, inventors, boat-builders and even the local bank managers of 30 years ago. The denouement of the story casts Robert Clifford, the man of action, as the great antagonist of an unholy cabal of money-men.

Predictably, the tale belongs also in the realms of social psychology and anthropology because the extraordinary events described are culturally determined to a substantial degree. You can't understand Robert Clifford and the extended Clifford family without an understanding of Tasmanian culture in particular, and island cultures in general. Tasmanians are maritime people who trade successfully with their own kind on a global basis.

And, it turns out, yachting culture also provides a template for a certain moment-to-moment way of doing business. It is a risky way of operating, but it is unusually agile. Both the risk and the agility have something to do with domination by a single 'skipper'. So, to an extent, this is also a biography of Tasmania—and of a quintessentially Tasmanian yachtsman.

And, as in all biographies, there is a family dimension. In the case of the Cliffords—Australians only since 1889—there are few indications of genius lurking in the dim past of the Clifford family in rural Gloucestershire and urban London. But they were always engaged in some form of manufacturing—and on their own behalf. So maybe there is something in the genes when it comes to making things in a businesslike fashion? And it certainly seems to be the case that the highly unconventional and volatile relationship between Robert Clifford and his butcher father helped to mould the character of the man himself. Nature or nurture? Probably both.

There is also much in these pages for the technology junkie. There is a fascination in the physics of the beautiful vessels manufactured in Hobart by the Cliffords. Their fitness-for-purpose depends on a very special marriage of materials science (the power-to-weight magic of aluminium) with sophistication of design and efficiencies of fuel consumption and carrying capacity. Bringing it all together looks much more like art than science.

We should never forget that working with natural materials to achieve something useful has a spiritual dimension too. We are programmed, as a species, to solve problems employing 'technology'. So the welders and others in the Hobart shipyard are happy and fulfilled in their work in a way that few employees are. If the Incat production facility ever migrates offshore, Hobart will have lost more than an economic engine—it will have lost part of its soul. In the wake of the global financial crisis, we now know that no economy can subsist on 'services' alone—and no human being finds ultimate satisfaction in 'work' without tangible value.

Technology-and-invention stories like this are usually of interest to economists too, because of the way that industrial 'clusters' habitually form around the nucleus of one 'mother ship' organisation with the power to connect with the outside world. Somebody like Robert Clifford doesn't just build an enterprise—he creates a kind of spume of supporting firms in the wake of the central ship-building activity. In so doing, he lifts those satellite firms to world-class performance standards and, in time, lifts the economy of the state and the nation too. The industrial 'cluster' thus becomes much more than the sum of its parts and the impact of the entrepreneur is widened.

Writing this account has been something of a labour of love. It is such an unlikely story. In order to capture this sense of improbability, I have called on the wisdom of the guru of professional storytelling—Robert McKee—because, as they say in journalism: 'You couldn't make it up!' It isn't a made-up story but it *sounds* like a made-up story. So it is a dramatic tale and, as McKee points out, the great tension in storytelling lies between plot and character—does plot mould character or does character drive the story forward? You can read this one either way. Robert Clifford is certainly one of the great 'characters', but it is hard to avoid the conclusion that this is an essentially event-driven tale.

So the book is a biography of sorts, but it is rather more than that—part social anthropology, part business school textbook, part educational treatise, part technology-innovation analysis, part economic geography—but mostly a ripping yarn about an adventurer. And, as Robert McKee might point out, we leave the story just at its most gripping moment—just before the end of the movie.

I toyed with the idea of entitling the book *A Perfect Australian?* on the grounds that Robert Clifford is not of course a perfect person, but his imperfections are those of the quintessential hard-bitten Australian of yore. The tough, taciturn, stubborn, individualistic battler in the outback wasn't meant to have any social graces, but he was supposed to be very ingenious in the face of challenge and adversity. And he was supposed to start with nothing and to triumph against the odds. He wasn't necessarily meant to be a sentimental bloke or to make a fortune. But you can't have everything.

In the end, I'm not sure these pages throw much light on the central mystery posed by Dick Smith: 'How did he do it?' The enterprise built from scratch by Robert Clifford over the course of 30 years is so complex, sophisticated and influential that it still seems improbable that one 'dunce', supported by immediate family and a group of loyal collaborators, could have made it happen. We are forced back to that imprecise notion of 'genius'.

PART ONE
Setting out

The young adventurer discovers his true *métier*

métier: a useful French word which describes both a
distinctive skill and a life's calling

1

Enter a genius

Robert Clifford was born in the middle of the World War in Hobart, Tasmania, on 3 February 1943—appropriately enough under the sign of Aquarius, seeing as he was to spend a lifetime in, on and around water. It was a dreadful three-day labour which his mother Eve was lucky to survive. He was the first-born, after prior miscarriages, and so he was much longed for and cherished. Eccentric from the start, he arrived on the scene with long white hair—looking a bit like an ancient Chinese priest. Usually, birth-hair falls out in due course—not young Robert's; his first visit to the barber was necessary at six months.

His father, christened Cecil Frederick but always known as Fred, was 31 when Robert was born, and 37 when the family was completed with the birth of Tony in 1949. The middle child Anne was born in 1945. Fred, as we shall see, was a key figure in the formation of the young entrepreneur. The Clifford stock was solidly English, coming originally from Swindon in Gloucestershire. By the late eighteenth century, a branch of the family was established at 9 Percival Street, Clerkenwell, in London and was engaged in modest commerce and jewellery manufacture. Somewhere in the genes may lie an appetite for making beautiful things—family-made heirloom jewellery still circulates in the extended Clifford family.

Robert Clifford is Australian only because there wasn't enough money for both of William Clifford's sons to enter the jewellery business, so the younger son Joseph decamped, as a Wesleyan missionary, to South Australia in 1889, along with his family—including his 19-year-old son Elijah. Thirteen years after their arrival, at 32 years of age, Elijah (who was Fred's father) married the 19-year-old Isabella Wade, a member of one of Melbourne's most established butchery families. They had 11 years of marriage before Elijah died (at 43) just as their seventh child was being born. At that time Elijah had risen to assistant stationmaster at Oakleigh in suburban Melbourne. Robert's father Fred was the sixth-born in 1912.

The redoubtable Isabella ('Jinny') then married George Thompson, a Scots-born baker, and bore him a further five children. The Clifford and Thompson progeny appear to have cohabited happily enough afterwards. With the early death of two infant Cliffords, George and Isabella were left with 10 children to bring up. So Fred, father and principal role model for Robert, grew up in the middle of a big, probably confusing and not-very-well-off family. And he never knew his true father. He was fetching balls on the local golf course from the age of six and caddying regularly not long afterwards. Later, Fred became a 'scratch' golfer (that is, a near-professional) and also excelled as a bicycle track racer. The Cliffords were seriously athletic.

At the age of 22, Fred decided to decamp to Tasmania—no one knows why. But his early entry into the butchery business in Hobart suggests some opportunism—after all, his mother's family were already well established in the trade. He was soon joined by his bride-to-be Eve Simmonds, and they started their 64-year marriage in 1937. A few years later, his young half-brother Alex Thompson joined them in Hobart. Fred and Alex were to remain a resourceful team of chancers and gamblers for the rest of their active lives—until, in fact, one of Fred's racing trotters kicked him in the chest in 1991. Fred was the entrepreneur and young Alex the bagman.

Eve came from a good solid Melbourne family and the Simmonds grandparents remained a loving and tranquil base for the Tasmanian Cliffords. The infant Robert travelled to Melbourne twice a year with his mother and it was mainly at the Simmonds' that Meccano entered the boy's life. The importance of this can't be overstated. But, if we look for signs of genius or unusual entrepreneurship in the Clifford or Simmonds family, we draw a blank—apart, perhaps, from the Clifford tradition of jewellery manufacture and Fred's bold decision to up stakes and move to Tasmania.

2

The making of an entrepreneur

When an extraordinary human being comes into the world, the psychologists usually want an explanation—and the explanation generally hinges around the old nature versus nurture argument. In other words, in February 1943—in the middle of a war—did a prescient midwife say (as they are known to do), 'Oh, you've got a right one there!' on the occasion of Robert Clifford's birth? If there was a midwife at all, she is not around to tell us what the infant Clifford was like on arrival and, anyway, she had an exhausted mother to cope with. The infant had contrived to survive a birth ordeal of unusual severity; it must have seemed a miracle at the time—especially in the light of Eve Clifford's earlier miscarriages in the five years since her marriage. It was, at any rate, a tough baby.

To ascertain whether or not Robert Clifford was born clever we need to examine the intellectual endowment of the parents. The biggest mistake this biographer ever made (in writing a chapter about Robert Clifford in 1997) was to accept at face value Fred Clifford's occupation as a butcher—or to quote one of the snob teachers at Hutchins School in Hobart, calling Fred 'just a butcher'.

Fred was indeed a butcher, but he was much more than that. Over the years, Fred became something of a serial entrepreneur—so he was possessed of the restless intellectual energy of a man who is impelled to find out what would happen if . . . or what could be made to happen if you . . . This is one form of cleverness that teachers don't always appreciate; it tends to disrupt orderly lessons in dead subjects. Young Robert was always close, or close enough, to Fred's business experiments to understand roughly what was being attempted.

One thing that became clear very quickly was that this baby seemed to have been born with unusual levels of ambition and stubborn determination. Of course, the determined baby requires a parent or parents more-or-less submissive to its will. The Clifford family folklore is replete with stories of the indomitable will of this particular baby. For example, once the regular visits to the barber became the norm, young Robert decided he could go to the barber on his own. This was when he was not yet three years of age and barely speaking. The barber was just around the corner and there were no roads to cross, but the exercise did require direct negotiation by the infant with the barber—which meant a mother, distraught with worry, shadowing the process all the way, just out of sight.

As a parent, you could say this was irresponsible and that the child should have been supervised more tightly. But, as Eve Clifford makes clear, there was no gainsaying this little one. So, unmindful of any danger, Robert made it to the barber on his own from then on and—more to the point—survived. Friends (and competitors) of the adult Clifford know all about this imperviousness to obstacles; it is not so much that the man sweeps obstacles aside—rather that he simply doesn't notice them in the first place. It is like a kind of autism when it comes to danger and risk.

So Robert was the target of what the psychologists call 'unconditional love'. It might be an exaggeration to say that he was the object of worship by his parents, but not a big exaggeration. When the siblings came along—Anne two years later and Tony after another four years—it was as if Robert had already sucked all the oxygen out of the family atmosphere. His younger siblings were loved as well and turned out wonderfully, but Robert remained the chosen one ('Only Robert had the birthday parties!'). So competition—an inconvenient fact most of us have to cope with—simply didn't register in this first-born's mental map. From a very early age, Robert Clifford expected to get his own way. As Eve recalls: 'He had to win!' If he had turned out to be a political tyrant, it might have mattered but, as we know, he became an inventor–genius on the side of good.

3

'The bastard's a genius'

But Robert's relationship with his father Fred was never straightforward or easy—in fact it was characterised, once Robert grew up a bit, by spectacular and semi-continuous brawling (metaphorically speaking). In Robert's memory, it was a 'boisterous' relationship. Fred had been hard on Robert from the start—but always with high expectations and Robert remembers that 'He was never satisfied.' It fell to Eve Clifford to be hard on the younger children Anne and Tony. Once Robert began to thrust himself (precociously) into the adult sphere, he began to disagree with Fred on just about everything—especially when it was clear to him Fred was getting things wrong. From the sidelines, it looked to astonished outsiders like undisciplined brawling; in reality, it seems to have been a continuous process of testing-out. Robert was learning to take charge and Fred was providing an apprenticeship in struggling for ascendancy. As Robert developed in ability and assertiveness, the key to the relationship lay in Fred's constant assertion: 'The bastard's a genius!'

Meanwhile, from his earliest infancy, Robert got to observe first-hand the supply chain involved in butchering, processing and bringing meat to market. By the age of four, he was even helping to make the sausages—quite an industrial process in itself. No four-year-old is ignorant of the *function* of a sausage; very few know exactly how sausages come into being. But the main Sandy Bay shop was just one of a chain of butchery outlets for which Fred was the buyer and ultimately head of syndicate; and he also had an interest in the abattoir 'upstream'. He took great pride in having built his own 'little empire' from not much at the war's end to a decent business when he retired in 1960. By then he had become Chairman of the Master Butchers' Association of Tasmania. He had never much liked butchery in the first place—having entered the trade at 22 and become 'sick of women complaining!' almost from the start.

Yet there was much more: the hire/drive car businesses Regal Sedans and Purdue Hire Cars; the Red Tulip chocolate agency and the lolly-making and distribution business; and the small goods supply business (including the sausages). None of these business ventures, however, seemed to have made much money; it wasn't until 1952 (when Robert was nine) that the family could afford to buy a house—and that a derelict farmhouse with a bit of land attached.

So, like a lot of entrepreneurs, Robert Clifford grew up in an atmosphere of financial unpredictability. The theory says that part of the explanation of the entrepreneurial personality lies in the need for *control*—the need to tame a naughty world, usually by accumulating money. To make matters worse, Fred and his younger half-brother and partner-in-crime Alex Thompson were inveterate gamblers. But not just gamblers—on Saturday mornings, the front room of the rented house in Sandy Bay was given over to the starting-price bookmaking business they ran on the side. It wasn't legal in those days (because they weren't buying the government gambling licence), but it was certainly a key element in Fred's business portfolio.

Of course, in that twilight world, collecting the money could be tricky. One of young Robert's earliest memories is of walking down the street with his father towards an oncoming gentleman; Fred said, 'See that bloke coming towards us—he'll cross the road before he gets to us.' And so it proved. All Robert knew then was that his father possessed an eerie kind of knowledge and power—along with a good many odd possessions in lieu of payment. Sometimes it worked that way in the butchery trade too, also notorious for unpaid bills. Fred got a brand new concrete garage built instead of payment for meat.

As you would expect of a businessman with an acute understanding of 'vertical integration'—or the control of a supply chain from top to bottom—Fred, as gambler, had to be in the upstream ownership and training of the racing animals, greyhounds and horses. It was said that the Clifford family always got the cheap cuts of meat from the butchery because the dogs had to have the best. Indeed, it was a 'trotter' that brought Fred's active business life to an end in 1991—by kicking him in the chest and condemning him to 11 years of relative incapacitation.

So, by the time he went to school, Robert had absorbed a great deal of business school type wisdom—about the management of supply chains, about manufacturing, about diversification of business interests and, above all, about *influence* or, as the business school might put it, *positioning*. On top of everything else (in a sports-mad country), Fred was a 'scratch' golfer at the local club. He was engaging in golfing contests with the good burghers of Hobart (whose wives were buying and cooking the best cuts of meat), and taking their surreptitious bets every Saturday—*that* is positioning! Fred's elder brother Bill became the professional at one of Melbourne's smarter golf clubs. And Fred had been a champion bicycle track racer in his youth; if there had been any money in it he might have made it his profession. Fred, in short, was a serious athlete.

4

Making, doing and invention

So much for the budding business entrepreneur. But there is something far more relevant to this story than entrepreneurship. At base, this is a story about invention: taking elements from nature and turning them into something entirely novel, akin to the design and building skills of his forebears in jewellery manufacture in Clerkenwell in the mid-nineteenth century. None of Robert Clifford's extraordinary achievement could have come into being without an obsessive need to understand how things are modelled and built—and a parallel skill in carrying through design-and-build ideas to fruition.

This went far beyond any nerdish little boy's desire to assemble the 'Airfix' kits designed by adults as children's toys. This was the need to make a near-perfect wooden model from a photograph of Sir Malcolm Campbell's racing car 'Bluebird'—from scratch. This little boy had been making elaborate models out of matchboxes at his granny's house in Melbourne since the age of three. Then, courtesy of granny, bits of Meccano kit began to appear until, at about eight years of age, the full Meccano set—heaven!

Readers today may not appreciate the importance of Meccano for generations of budding scientists and engineers. The great chemist and Nobel Laureate Professor Sir Harry Kroto understands:

I had Meccano and I had this world in which I did things. Toys are one thing but toys are only a stepping-stone to reality. Meccano is somewhere between a toy and a real piece of engineering equipment. My father used Meccano to set up gigs and make things in the factory—the point being that you could use it for pilot structures. The sad thing is that Meccano has all but disappeared, so kids no longer get the chance to develop the skills of nuts and bolts and the way things are actually built. It's about what feeling for materials you get—what feelings for structures; triangulation of joints; what fundamental geometric structures are important for stability. Nobody learns things without actually doing things! ('The Meccano Man', *New Humanist*, vol. 117, issue 1, 2002)

It's no surprise that Sir Harry is contemptuous of modern formal education, believing that important innate skills like language acquisition, analytic ability and abstract thought tend to fall away after the first three or four years of life—long before schools tackle them. So he would be unsurprised that another great Meccano enthusiast (Robert Clifford) should fail at the formal aspects of school and only come good again when presented with complicated constructional problems in the real world. As Sir Harry says:

Perhaps the only ability I have is a determination to do things as well as possible. I'm not a great scientist in comparison to some people who are fantastic theoretically. But I understand these things, I have certain abilities and I put things together in a way that is sometimes better than other people. I do something. I just do it single-mindedly! (ibid.)

So what the famous Nobel Laureate says about his own work and creativity might have come from the lips of Robert Clifford—he just took a different path. But the starting point was Meccano—getting clever by making and doing. Sir Harry shares other traits with his contemporary Clifford—an artistic sensibility and a love of high-demand sporting endeavour. They might enjoy swapping notes: Clifford would understand Kroto-style chemistry (he began to learn serious materials science as soon as Incat got into aluminium) and Kroto would certainly appreciate the latest 112-metre fast catamarans—very big, very fast, very complex Meccano assemblies.

There should be some kind of correlative research on the impact of Meccano on the development of outstanding creatives, based on the insight that a serious absorption in the work of making, modelling and building causes people to become very clever indeed—irrespective of their prowess in ordinary schoolwork. It comes as no surprise that another of Australia's most creative people and another contemporary, the entrepreneur Dick Smith, was—from the age of about five—a Meccano fanatic. This would be most valuable educational research—testing the hypothesis that Meccano (as an easily identifiable independent variable ubiquitous in the 1940s) doesn't just make you handy (*Homo habilis*) it makes you clever (*Homo sapiens*). The more eccentric forms of 'action research' might be employed to film the interaction of Robert Clifford, Sir Harry Kroto and Dick Smith around a really complicated Meccano set. The trait common to these three individuals is not that they are clever, but that they also make of lots of things happen—they are tremendous net contributors to society in their different ways.

At any rate, Robert Clifford's earliest schooldays were not happy because his gifts were non-standard. The family was still living in rented flats—Robert slept in an alcove. And he was badly bullied at the tough Prince's Street School. But, mercifully, he began to grow big fast—and a naturally pugnacious temperament came to his rescue. A good part of his awkwardness must have flowed from the basic curriculum: he had come to school from a quasi-adult role in the Clifford family enterprise, helping in a small way to run a rather complex, supply chain-based business, and acutely aware of a range of other enterprises on the side. And, to cap it all, he was a very slow reader—dyslexic like a great many spatial prodigies and, more to the point, entirely without interest in the contents of textbooks. From his earliest schooldays, he adopted the practice of copying all his homework—the punishment being clearly less onerous than the homework itself. In modern business parlance, copying your homework might be looked on as intelligent 'partnering'; anyway, that's how young Clifford looked on it.

Everything changed at the start of 1954, when Robert (predictably) failed the Schools' Board examinations to get into the academic high school in Hobart. This coincided with Fred's great success in winning the famous (in dog-racing circles) 'Hobart 1000' race with his greyhound Pasha Chief (the prize at that time was a munificent Stg£1300—about A$15 000–A$20 000 in today's money). There is no direct causal link between this event and Robert's subsequent enrolment in the private Church of England boys' school Hutchins—established in 1846 for the sons of gentlemen—but it signifies a decisive shift into the middle-class world for the butcher/bookmaker with high aspirations for his 'genius' son. Neither of Robert's younger siblings Anne or Tony went to private schools—that was Robert's job for the Clifford clan. Indeed, Fred had actually fantasised about Geelong Grammar (Australia's Eton and not even in Tasmania) for his elder son.

5

Education and 'intelligence'

This is the moment to reflect on the nature of formal education, especially for gifted youngsters like Robert Clifford, who have developed their high intelligence mainly by making and doing—that is, in the same way as young human infants had always done before the advent of these strange institutions we call schools. As Sir Harry Kroto points out, formal schooling actually gets in the way of our species' natural development. Professor Howard Gardner of Harvard has devoted much of his distinguished academic career to understanding how the human brain is wired and to examining how, if at all, our approach to education is aligned with our natural processes of learning (*Frames of Mind*, 1983).

Gardner, famously, drew attention to the different types of 'intelligences' (plural) we are heir to. He based some of this analysis on studies of brain damage, which show us the different physical locations in the neural circuitry of particular capabilities. Each of these capabilities is clearly useful to us (that's why they are 'hard-wired' in our brains), but not all are universally understood or appreciated by schoolteachers. If, as infant, you turn out to be good at the 'linguistic' and the 'logico-mathematical' skills, you are likely to be dubbed 'bright' by both parents and teachers. In all likelihood, demonstrated ability in language and computation is what causes many schoolteachers to get into teaching in the first place.

If, like young Clifford, you don't read at all and your mathematical skills turn out, much later, to be geometrical rather than arithmetical, then you may not be appreciated fully by conventional teachers. If, further, you disdain all schoolwork and copy everything from compliant friends, then you may come to be regarded not just as a dunce, but as a rather uncooperative one at that. If your true genius is to be found in another two of the 'intelligences' described by Gardner—namely, the 'spatial' and the 'bodily-kinaesthetic'—then you will probably need at least one teacher who grew up using Meccano and who understands that there is an entirely different, and very powerful, intelligence to be found in people who can 'see' at a glance how the world is arranged and who can move gracefully to order. (Gardner points out the gifts of outstanding athletes and dancers are not located in their limbs but in the rich feedback loops between limbs and brain (ibid.).) One of the teachers at Hutchins actually said to Robert: 'You'll never amount to anything—you're just the son of a butcher!' Whatever happened to that teacher?

So young Robert set off to posh Hutchins School—one of three such schools in Hobart—the others were Quaker-run and Roman Catholic. Going to Hutchins entailed five years of half-hour journeys over the Derwent River every day, usually accompanied by Bill 'Wobbler' Reid—another of the not-so-posh boys whose parents had managed to get him into a 'good' school. This was 10 years before Hobart got a proper bridge crossing over the river; the ferry service was thus an essential lifeline for inhabitants of the rapidly expanding eastern suburbs. When the big bridge finally opened in 1964, it destroyed the ferry service. So when Robert Clifford revived the ferry service in 1972, he was (in business parlance) well 'positioned' for the destruction of the bridge in 1975, but that is another story, for later.

As young Clifford didn't get on with the Hutchins curriculum or discipline, he was not wildly popular with most of the teachers. But he got on well enough with his companions in the B class of non-academic types. The A class had about 40 bright kids drawn mostly from Tasmania's 'old' money or from professional families; the B class had just 16 or so supposed dullards. Maybe the small class size helped, because the B class seems to have produced all the successful entrepreneurs—those youngsters who already knew how to make and do—rather than how to study and pass exams. Some of them probably grasped that the curriculum was supremely irrelevant for their likely adult lives. Robert barely *noticed* the curriculum. Other well-known schoolboy 'dullards'—like Winston Churchill ('the stupidest boy at Harrow')—often turn out to be people who were not stupid at all but who disdained the formal regime of school, who simply refused to go along with it.

By this time, the young Robert was firmly established under the sobriquet 'Bean' or 'Big Bean'—the name dating from his first day at Bellerive Primary School when someone called the ten-year-old a 'Big Bean'. The name stuck. For some reason, all persons of substance in that wartime generation required a peculiar nickname. Presumably, no nickname meant no status at all. No one knows how Wobbler came by his. Eventually, Robert Clifford became a person of great international substance—a holder of the Order of Australia and possessor of an array of honorary university degrees—but in Hobart he remained, and remains to this day, 'Beanhead'.

6

'Giftedness' and the 'crystallising' moment

Back in the 1940s, nobody much bothered about 'giftedness' in young children. Nowadays, there is a substantial industry surrounding the identification of giftedness and the reinforcement of parents' deeply ingrained belief that their child is special. Even if the 'gifted' notion had had any currency back then, there is no certainty that anybody (save for Fred) would have spotted anything positive in Robert Clifford's quirky persona. Fred, who must have been gifted himself, always knew the bastard was a genius. The latest research suggests that it really does take one to know one; the gifted child surrounded by normal kids just seems strange—just 'too much'—hyper-attuned to external sensation, restless, perfectionistic, scarily intense and subject to 'asynchronous' development (racing ahead in development of one skill or another). But surround the gifted child with its own kind and everybody gets on fine because they understand each other.

It is clear from Eve Clifford's vivid memories of the young Robert that he came into the world with that characteristic pattern of high cognitive capability nowadays referred to as giftedness. From the start, he was super-aware and super-reactive to his environment (even the barber around the corner) and demonstrated a precocious need to persevere and to perfect objects of work (the matchbox inventions, for example). Kids like this are very intense (excitable and sensitive), complex (perceptive and original thinkers) and driven (creative in a productive way—always working away at something engrossing). Because they are perceived by other children as strange, they tend to adopt one of two tactics to ease their way into society: either they go into a kind of lock-down—restraining their natural energy and curiosity so as to seem normal or as 'thick' as everybody else; or they go to the other extreme by exaggerating brashness, over-the-topness and indiscipline. From all accounts, this was Robert Clifford's stratagem—if he couldn't be normal (that is, dull) he would be in-your-face. Of course it helps, in a sports-mad country, to be a natural athlete and to grow big and strong. So he found a way of concealing his embarrassing genius from everybody (except Fred). And Fred indulged his natural intensity, complexity and drive by demanding ever higher standards and by brawling with him creatively.

•

This part of the book kicked off with a definition of the French word '*métier*'. It's all very well to be a genius (that is, specially gifted at something or other), but at some point those gifts have to be channelled into a 'calling'—some activity that the individual was clearly 'meant' to pursue. They say in the world of the specially gifted that the child doesn't find the 'right track', the right track finds the child—if he or she is lucky. Those daily ferry trips across the Derwent were important for the youngster already experienced in managerial operations and butchery supply chains. It was inevitable he would take an interest in the operation of the ferries and in the organisation behind them—in the *system*. His school friend Wobbler reports that one day on the ferry, Robert actually said: 'One day, I'm going to run ferries over the Derwent! . . . One day, I'll have boats that go over Bass Strait and all over the world.' This was around 1956 when Robert was 13 years old. As career aspirations go, it doesn't get more precise than that. But Wobbler's central role in the Clifford story dates from an earlier conversation in 1955 (Robert was 12) when Wobbler put out the call: 'I need a crew on Saturday!'

Wobbler had an 11-foot sailing dinghy which he raced on Saturdays. Up until that point, Robert Clifford, a champion swimmer, had never got his hands on a sailing boat. Once he did, courtesy of Wobbler, he was away. Howard Gardner calls this moment the 'crystallising experience'—the moment when a young person (maybe an academic non-achiever) suddenly discovers what he was meant by fate to do—what he is *for* (*Frames of Mind*, 1983). It turned out Robert Clifford was a superb helmsman and astute reader of the conditions surrounding the progress of a yacht through water. That is what the spatial and bodily-kinaesthetic intelligences equip you for. And he learned fast what all entrepreneurs need to learn eventually that (in yacht racing as in life): 'There is no such thing as a postponed decision because in 10 minutes' time it's a different decision!'

This insight, by the way, is the key to effective and timely decision-making in all situations of great uncertainty and ambiguity. It also provides the explanation for the most spectacular business cockups—when big decisions are delayed disastrously or plunged into precipitately. As the social scientist Professor Gillian Stamp puts it: 'Judgement is what you do when you don't know what to do (but you sense you'd better do something pretty soon)!' (*Brief Notes on Capability*, 1988).

And, of course, the skill of a great helmsman is not physically located in the 'seat of the pants'—any more than the skill of a dancer or athlete is located in the legs—it is located somewhere between limbs (or posterior) and *brain*. As Howard Gardner points out, it is a special form of 'bodily-kinaesthetic' *intelligence* of particular usefulness to anybody required to respond to a physical challenge in the natural world (*Frames of Mind*, 1983). If that challenge involves, for example, hunting animals on the veldt as our earliest ancestors had to, then the 'spatial' intelligence is going to be handy as well—because it permits the hunter on the ground to 'see' the terrain as if from a helicopter. The Shell Company dubbed this strategic capacity 'helicopter vision' back in the 1970s and pronounced it the key determinant of promotion to the highest levels in the firm. We all possess these gifts but some do so prodigiously. Robert Clifford, the son of an exceptional athlete, is one of them.

When I devoted a chapter ('The Ingenious "Dunce"') to Robert Clifford in my 1997 book *Intelligent Leadership*, I made two errors in an otherwise accurate picture of the Incat saga to that date. The first was to accept at face value Fred Clifford's occupation as a butcher. As we have seen, that was true but woefully incomplete—Fred was much more than 'just a butcher'. The other error was suggesting that Hutchins, as a well-endowed, riverside private school, had a sailing program among its offerings. I imagined that Hutchins might have anticipated Gardner's writings on 'multiple intelligence' and provided a comprehensive curricular menu which fed all the intelligences. The truth was more mundane. There was no Hutchins sailing 'program' as such—indeed, the headmaster was firmly anti-sailing, on the grounds that it tended to lead to alcohol consumption (he was right about that). The real value of Hutchins to Robert Clifford's future was the presence of other boys with fathers rich enough to finance a dinghy or two.

Gardner's point about the 'crystallising experience' is that children who don't read (or who seem not to be able to) sometimes become avid readers overnight when they have something really interesting to read *about*. Thus Robert Clifford was crystallised by helmsmanship, and once he became a serious sailor himself he began to read everything about racing technique, sail design, navigation and so on. If you are going to build a A$200 million business in just 40 years, you are going to have to start reading at some point.

Thirteen years of age is quite late to start reading but evidently not too late. Without the stimulus of Wobbler's dinghy, Robert Clifford the entrepreneur might never have emerged. As Gardner says: 'IQ tests would be completely different if they were designed by entrepreneurs' (*Frames of Mind*, 1983).

All this has significance for education policy, of course. If every public school in the land were as affluent as Hutchins (and every pupil cohort as polyglot as that post-war class of 1954), then more talented odd-ball children like Robert Clifford might be produced for national wealth creation (or, in some cases, spared jail). And of course, if you don't feed the appetite for making and doing, there is always the likelihood that ingenious make-and-do youngsters will turn their ingenuity to subversion of their school. When this happens, the kids who fail in the linguistic and logico-mathematical fields are likely to utilise their interpersonal and spatial skills to destabilise the entire school—for fun. The interpersonal intelligence allows them to provoke teachers just to the point of apoplexy (but not beyond), and the spatial intelligence allows them to model the power system of the school so as to manipulate it.

7

The first boat

Once water became Robert Clifford's principal medium—ferrying to school on it, swimming (competitively) in it and speeding over it in small boats—school life divided itself into two compartments: enduring (or possibly eluding) the formal aspects; and turning the school system to practical make-and-do use. By 14 years of age, Robert had built his first boat (a 14-foot skate) in his parents' house. Getting the thing out on completion involved luring his mother away for the day in order to demolish and rebuild a section of the house. It was meant to be a woodworking project at Hutchins, and Robert was given a fail grade because the teachers couldn't believe he'd built the boat himself.

Not long after, Fred impulse-bought a 25-foot 'Derwent' class yacht for young Robert to race on the river. In theory, he was far too young to take on the adults racing these craft in fierce competition: in practice, he was growing big fast and learning to stand his ground pugnaciously. And Fred knew, after all, that the bastard was a genius. Naturally, Robert also built a meticulous model of the 'D-class'. Owning the yacht entailed a self-managed crash-course in sail design and manufacture. This meant spending every school lunch hour hanging out at an indulgent sailmaker's, thinking through spinnaker design and the merits of materials (cotton/Terylene/Dacron/nylon) and the theory of deeper sail pockets—'I had my own ideas on spinnaker shapes!' Over the next few years, he completely redesigned the backstays and runners, the mast control strop and anything else likely to increase speed in the water—pushing the strict yacht-racing rules to the limits. The Japanese call this principle *kaizen*, or 'continuous incremental improvement'. Management consultants still try to teach the discipline of *kaizen* to big firms; Robert Clifford knew all this by the age of 15.

The school was ignorant of young Robert's maritime achievements. In fact, the young Robert was learning how to solve a complex problem (winning races in unpredictable conditions) by co-opting or coercing more or less willing suppliers to the cause. Years later, one of Incat's main claims to fame was its creation of a network of long-term supplier partners—now known by government and academia alike as the 'Tasmanian Light Shipbuilding Cluster'. He was already learning how to create a kind of industrial 'cluster' in 1957. Indeed, his approach to getting his homework assignments completed (copying from friends) can be seen as a logical extension of this supply-side logic. Teachers call it 'cheating'; any sensible manufacturer calls it creative partnership.

Around this time, Eve Clifford got a new sewing machine as a 'present' from her adoring son. It was equipped, of course, with sailmaker's stitching and used for nothing else afterwards. If Hutchins had laid on a sailing program and an associated educational support, they could have laid claim to very advanced educational thinking for that large minority of pupils wired-up for making and doing. Howard Gardner would have been impressed. As it was, Robert Clifford was learning how to build a A$200 million business on the side.

Hutchins got a look in again when Robert took on the stage management aspects of the school's production of Gilbert and Sullivan's *Ruddigore* in 1958. The art teacher did most of the painting but the 15-year-old took charge of much of the set design and building and, crucially, the co-ordination of the production. The excitement of that collaborative experience left a deep impression on him: he was learning a lot about teamwork and a bit about leadership in a setting of unpredictability. There are plenty of schoolchildren for whom 'peripheral' events like the school play turn out to be the central educational experience of their young lives.

At any rate, by the end of that year he had left school, before his sixteenth birthday. Hutchins, despite itself, had offered all it could. Robert Clifford, arguably an 'adult' ever since he helped to manufacture sausages as a four-year-old, was good and ready for the adult world. Leaving school early (without a diploma) was important only in the sense that it shielded him from orthodoxy. Years later he remarked: 'If I had received a regular education, I might now be building regular ships!' In other words, he never learned what he *couldn't* do.

It's worth noting, as we are addressing the matter of entrepreneurship, that Robert Clifford's early entrepreneurial activity was entirely animated by creative problem-solving. He was not, like many budding 'entrepreneurs', out on the street with a homemade lemonade stand or selling second-hand electronic goods to his school chums to make a few dollars. The word 'entrepreneur' means, in rough translation from the French, *enterpriser*—one who finds out what can be done with any particular situation in order to transform it into something else. Robert's father Fred had that restless need to find out what can be made to happen—but nearly always in the context of trying to make some money. Robert Clifford inherited the same curiosity but in a purer and non-commercial form. His enterprises were essentially *scientific*—finding out for its own sake how to make the perfect spinnaker shape so as to solve a weight, wind-capture, surface-tension/friction problem in the real world—to make a yacht go faster. Sir Harry Kroto (see p. 13) would understand.

8

Testing the
employment waters

Fred was determined that after Robert quit school he should have a trade and establish a good working habit. After a few false starts, the lad ended up apprenticed as a compositor to Jack Newman, the owner of Specialty Press of Hobart. He spent two and a half years there and managed on the way to win the 'Apprentice of the Year' award. He loved operating the old linotype machines, but could see from the start that the local newspaper was already switching over from hot metal to the new photographic printing methods. Also Mr Newman had two children coming into the business, so printing was a blind alley on the career and technical front for a young man whose *métier* was really water. But it wasn't a blind alley from a learning perspective because young Robert got to see at first hand how to build a small firm into a much bigger one by being sensible and looking after the customers—an important lesson.

Jack Newman became a kind of reserve father to the young Robert. There were no shouting matches, just a mutually respectful relationship between a paternal sort of older man and a very bright youngster eager to learn. Newman very likely spotted that the lad really was 'gifted'—he certainly offered to double his pay to keep him in the business. The employment relationship matured into a long-term friendship and, until Jack's death in the 1980s, he would always be asked along on delivery voyages of the various vessels that Incat manufactured. Robert Clifford still regards Jack Newman as the only true 'boss' he ever had, perhaps because he felt understood and fully appreciated. One legacy of his time in the printing trade was a residual belief in his expertise in anything to do with printing and publishing, and Incat eventually became a major publisher of trade and marketing materials.

A significant by-product of those two years in the printing trade was an enduring enthusiasm for the principle of apprenticeship. The appeal is obvious for a young man who has failed academically but who comes alive when presented with the chance to design or make something useful in the real world. Howard Gardner's definition of intelligence is actually: 'The ability to solve a problem or fashion a product that is valued in at least one culture or community' (*Frames of Mind*, 1983). So it comes as no surprise that, when Robert was in a position to create a learning system to make better ships, he not only installed a superior apprenticeship system, but he also invented an upstream technical college to educate and support *his* apprentices.

9

Back to the water

In 1960, aged 48, Fred decided to 'retire'—at any rate from the butchery trade. He had never much liked it but he had worked hard in the 15 years since the war to build up his 'little empire'. The business fetched 28 000 pounds in the old currency (something like $700 000 Australian dollars now). He had brought his family through from near poverty to a kind of middle-class respectability, even allowing for the déclassé bookmaking and gambling. But any idea of Fred retreating to the golf course went straight out the window as, almost immediately, he signed up for his elder son's passion for boat-building and yacht racing—supporting Robert's grand plan to build a 30-foot Van de Stadt-designed 'Black Soo' yacht in the back garden. The plan was to 'go ocean racing'.

Robert, still in the printing business, really needed to get back on the water. In retrospect, it is entirely possible that he would have become a professional international yacht racer if that particular career had opened up 10 years earlier; just as Fred, likewise, felt he might have become a professional bicycle track racer if that career had offered the prospect of money in the 1930s. They settled for sailing together. The Black Soo never got finished; it was sold part-constructed when a new wheeze took over—Fred decided, more or less overnight, to 'go fishing'. Robert had no particular interest in fishing as a career, but he viewed it as a way of making a living and it did offer the prospect of a life on the water. Also he carried a deeply entrenched presumption that Fred might get it wrong without his (Robert's) guidance. By then, they had more or less completed the father–son role-reversal that Fred seems to have envisioned from the start.

So, aged 19, Robert went into business with his dad. We can regard the two and a half years apprenticeship in the printing trade as the completion of his education; it taught him at least that he wasn't really the employee type. Going fishing truly meant entry into the adult world—and in a very challenging and uncertain trade. This was a true enterprise so Fred and Robert became entrepreneurs. It's worth reviewing how equipped the young man was for entrepreneurship.

To begin with, he seems to have been born energetic and determined so this must have been inherited from someone or other. And part of his genetic endowment seems to be the physical co-ordination of the top-class athlete. More important still is the aptitude for the manipulation of models and the invention of new devices. Indeed, this looks very like a compulsion—the only way for a Robert Clifford to be happy in life is to be engaged in invention and creation. Whether or not it makes any money is a side issue. And, crucially, he had learned to be competitive through all the yacht racing; he would never shirk a fight. Above all, it looks as though had he been born 50 years later, some educational psychologist might have labelled him 'gifted'.

The fishing enterprise started off with Fred's impulse purchase of *Narracoopa*—a large, clapped-out trading vessel. His idea was to adapt it as a 'mother ship' to a fleet of smaller boats fishing for salmon. Fred was still thinking in supply chain terms—like a butcher with interests in an upstream abattoir and a downstream retail outlet. He had got wind of the fact that small New South

Wales-based fishing boats had discovered vast reserves of salmon in Tasmanian waters, and were hauling in 60 or 70 tonnes of fish on every trip. Their problem was getting the catch to market, so the refrigerated 'mother ship' concept made a kind of 'systems thinking' sense, provided you could integrate its movements with the satellite boats. Fred ended up buying small boats to keep *Narracoopa* busy—the tail wagging the dog.

Robert was still in the printing trade when Fred launched this venture and it was already in trouble when the youngster stepped in to lend a hand—or put a stop to the haemorrhage of money. Robert actually ended up building the freezers on board. They made the enterprise work as well as possible but two years later, when the ship was sold, Fred had lost all his retirement money on the enterprise. They had, however, learned a lot on the way: conceptually, it made sense, but the execution was ill thought out.

Despite their financial losses, the Cliffords stayed on in the fishing business. They were operating and continuously adapting a series of boats, mainly designed to catch and process crayfish. Tasmania has about 65 workable days per year for crayfish fishing, much of it in the wild waters of the 'roaring forties' on the west coast, so it's important for productivity that all the processes are efficient. And the boats have to be adaptable to prawning and scalloping in the northern states in the winter months—a variation on the supply chain logic of the butchery business. For the next few years, Robert's creative juices were used up in first adapting boats for greater efficiencies and then designing and building new kinds of boats from scratch.

Robert Clifford the inventor was immediately engaged by the back-breaking and dangerous labour of emptying heavy scallop dredges by hand. For more than 50 years, the traditional rig had been a flat platform on the back of the boat with an overhead gantry. It required two or three men to climb the platform after the swinging dredge was landed and to bend down and tip out the contents. It would have been tricky in any seas, but it was truly hazardous in the rough.

Clifford started, as usual, by making small models from balsawood and pins of a new system for tipping. Then he installed on one boat a prototype of a self-tipping dredge system which eliminated the need for the gantry completely. The final version was then installed on another of his boats, an adapted 97-year-old schooner called *Gazelle*. It was easy, very efficient and, above all, safe. Within a very short time, it had become a standard piece of equipment on all such fishing vessels. Even today, all scallop-tipping boats use the same system, virtually as invented by Robert Clifford in 1964. Once again, Clifford was practising both *kaizen* and the arts of the inventor.

Meanwhile, the Cliffords' fishing business was more or less flourishing, but the constant financial demands of technical innovation and the vagaries of fishing itself meant that the business always teetered on the edge of solvency. On a good day, you might land 81 dozen crayfish and 150 bags of scallops—that would be a hugely profitable catch. A good week-long trip might yield 4.5 tonnes of crayfish. But one three-month trip to the Gulf of Carpentaria in northern Australia ended up with a total catch of two prawns. This way of life was demanding, always dangerous because they took risks in pursuit of profit, and totally absorbing.

10

A family man

In the middle of all this, Robert got married. He had met the redoubtable Barbara Deegan in 1963 when she was the reigning 'Miss Derwent' and they married on 2 January 1965. He was 21 and she was 20. They were too young, no doubt, and they produced two wonderful children (both now directors of Incat), but the reason for the seemingly inevitable split-up five years later and divorce (finalised 12 years later) was that, although Barb no doubt thought she was marrying a lovely, charismatic bloke (she was), the truth was she was marrying an enterprise. True entrepreneurs like Robert Clifford are inseparable from their creations. And she had joined the enterprise just at the point when her new husband was almost totally absorbed in one of the most demanding and dangerous businesses in the world.

For the next few years Barb had to put up with 16 different houses in 18 months accompanied by two infant children. She would find herself cooking for 20 fishermen (the 'strays and misfits' whom the Cliffords habitually collected around their central enterprise) drawn from a half-dozen Tasmanian fishing boats following wherever Robert led. The first child, Craig, was born during the first scallop fishing trip to Bermagui in southern New South Wales. Kim was born in the same year as *Leillateah*—a 45-foot wooden craft which was built to replace another (non-Clifford) boat lost in a storm. Kim came into the world during another Bermagui fishing trip. This was par for the course because the timing, according to the family version, depended on the fishing—Craig and Kim were both born, two years apart, exactly nine months after the opening of the fishing season. When the fishing was in season, during their infancy the kids were as likely to bunk up on board a boat as on shore and the various fisherfolk acted as a kind of extended family when it came to childcare. They were much loved but they were certainly not mollycoddled.

In a way, the Clifford marriage was a casualty of Robert's discovery of the only working scallop-bed in New South Wales—a discovery assisted by relatively high-tech depth sounding. Having employed science to find the scallops in the first place, the Cliffords set to work to exploit the remarkable opportunity. There wasn't much time to devote to the marriage, as such. In the end, they semi-permanently employed a local driver (his private life disappeared too) to run a refrigerated van all up and down the coast, with incursions to Canberra, in order to sell the precious scallops to restaurateurs and the more advanced domestic cooks. Thus a small van emblazoned with the legend 'Lanzing Scallops' became the public (marketing) face of F.C. Clifford Pty Ltd and of the 27-year-old Robert. That, the textbooks tell us, is pretty much the entrepreneurial personality at work—constantly exploring, employing all means (including science) to exploit opportunities, and ruthlessly penetrating (or creating) markets. There is not much time left over for new wives and infants; the kids at any rate seem to have loved all the excitement. Barbara finally 'walked' in 1970.

The next great romantic love of Robert's life came on the scene five years later in 1975 and was actually the first employee of the newly formed International Catamarans Pty Ltd in 1977. So Kerry Sturmey, latterly a director of the firm, knew what she was getting into; not a bloke *or* a company—but the two conjoined. By the time they began to live together he was 34 and she was 29 so it was a grown-up relationship from the start—and it endured. In the meantime, the kids were brought up by their mother in a set-up much more reminiscent of Bohemian Paris than straitlaced Hobart. Craig and Kim had the benefits of a mother's love, plus a kind of wise reserve mother in Kerry, and Robert was freed up to pursue his dreams. It was unusual, but it worked. After the separation, Barbara set up a bed and breakfast business almost immediately, so the children never knew any other kind of parent but the very busy, working kind. Later on, she upsized to a substantial backpacker B&B with 26 rooms.

Meanwhile, the various extended families stepped in to share the childcare. Craig spent much of his infancy with his much-loved maternal grandparents and Kim tended to stick with her mother. But Robert was always there, though his idea of sharing with the kids was to assume they were as interested in boat-building as he was; there was no going to the park or playground or suchlike, but you might get to go sailing with lots of beer, laughs, girls and swearing. Not a bad trade-off for the wide-eyed young Craig. Barbara's parents were sad about the marriage breakdown but they could see, everybody could see, that Robert was basically married to the business of inventing, designing and making boats. That was just the way it was.

There is a respectable body of theory to suggest an intermingling of professional and personal life in driven and highly creative men. The psychologist Professor Liam Hudson (working with his wife Bernadine Jacot) studied the biographies of very eminent scientists (an entry in *Who's Who* was the qualification) in different fields. It turned out that eminent male chemists tended to stay married to the same woman for a lifetime, although not necessarily to lavish much attention on her (the work is the thing). Eminent physicists were much more likely to a pursue a metamorphic passage through a series of women and/or marriages—the more eminent, the more women/marriages. But Hudson detected a correlation between breakthroughs in the work and the destruction of old relationships ('Fertility in the Arts and Sciences', *Social Studies of Science*, vol. 3, 1973, pp. 305–10). True breakthroughs in physics generally involve destruction of old paradigms—and they coincide with eruptions in personal life. Robert Clifford, a physicist in all but name, only married the once ('I'm not doing that again!') but never lost the creative impulse nor the loving nature of the much-loved child he had once been. To the outside world he was the tough guy; those closer to home know better.

In 1964, something else happened which was to have an important bearing on this tale of entrepreneurship: the new Tasman Bridge over the River Derwent was finally opened to traffic. This was a major contribution to Hobart's infrastructure—the Derwent is a wide river and a lot of development had occurred on the eastern shore—including the city's access to the airport. The bridge it replaced was narrow and had to keep lifting a span to allow ships through. The impact of the new high-span bridge on the existing ferry services was immediate and unhelpful. The bridge straightaway sucked in traffic and so became a key 'choke-point' in Hobart communications. Suddenly, a quarter-million population city had a dependency on a single, major river crossing.

11

From fishing
to ferrying

Between 1962 and 1972, the Cliffords built or adapted a total of five boats—the last two of which, *Lanzing* and *Leillateah*, were wooden boats constructed from Robert's novel designs to solve a series of technical problems. One innovation was a pumped system around the boat's 'well' (for the live crayfish) to increase the height of the well and provide a heating/cooling circulation system around the crew's bunks. The ships designed for the wild west coast had reinforced hulls, bigger holds for more powerful diesel engines and 'powerful bilges, capable of carrying a good load of fish a long distance' (from interview with Robert Clifford, 2004; correspondence, 2008). Another innovation was depth-sounding to find the crayfish. This was *kaizen* with a vengeance—the constant search for useful innovation in the service of performance.

While established Hobart boat-builders did the construction, the young designer was in charge of all purchasing and finance and, subsequently, the on-board fitout (because they never had the luxury of completing a boat before the next fishing season came upon them). In a way, this resembles the 'just-in-time' scheduling of Japanese manufacturing. In Clifford's case, it was a necessity—getting the semi-finished boat out on the water to catch the crayfish to pay the 30-day accounts: 'We launched her on the Wednesday, went to sea on the Sunday and 12 days later we had a full load of crayfish!'

This could be a close-run thing: if he had not succeeded in catching the height of the crayfish season, he could not have repaid the A$10 000 borrowed to fund the construction of one boat. As it was, one creditor had already sent in the bailiffs to repossess his refrigerator by the time they got back to port. By now, he had learned to keep creditors waiting 'nicely' but always to pay the bank. So, in his twenties, Robert had become a combination of research and development, finance, marketing, 'lean' (just-in-time) manufacturing and operations. He was also the principal labourer on site. He had become a one-man business, without going to university at all—and all to bail his father out of a rash business venture. He had learned to sail 'close to the wind' in business as well as in sailing.

Long before the end of the fishing business in 1972, Robert had lost heart with it—with the constant absences from home and family, and with battling the atrocious weather on Tasmania's west coast. It had destroyed his marriage and he had run out of fishing boat innovations. It had not, however, destroyed his passion for water, shipping and ship-building. And the long periods of inactivity on the boats provided the chance to catch up on reading—any reading was good enough for the ex-'dunce'. As the construction of the new Tasman bridge had led to the closing down of the ferry service, he harboured a desire to start it up again—this time with a bit of pizazz. The business concept was that the Derwent River is much more than an obstacle to the daily commuter; it is one of the loveliest stretches of water in the world which happens to be located in a tourist trap. And Robert was wise enough to sense that he needed more in life: 'My mind was too active; I wanted to get into the ferryboat business!'

So the business school take on the Sullivan's Cove Ferry Company (set up in 1972) is that it aimed to exploit the leisure potential of

Hobart's waterway, as well as reintroduce a ferry service for that part of the population which will always prefer to commute without recourse to driving. A close observer of Robert Clifford's form might have observed a good excuse to build another boat. The Cliffords had come to the end of the fishing design-and-build road. The challenge now was to design and build a craft specifically for the Derwent River—a 'Trans-Derwent Ferry' for combined ferry and leisure activity.

The Sullivan's Cove Ferry Company (SCFC) was in fact a business alliance of the Cliffords (father and son), Barbara (now separated from Robert and working hard at two jobs to get her stake in the business) and a group of interested locals, including a surgeon and an accountant. The sale of the fishing boats funded (just) the construction of the *Matthew Brady*—a 70-foot all-steel ferry designed and built in collaboration with a local marine construction firm and named, like all the ships to follow, after infamous Tasmanian bushrangers. The hull was built by another self-taught boat-builder and academic failure who actually left school at 12! Trevor Hardstaff ended up as Incat's production director.

The Clifford marriage was unusual in that husband and wife went into business together only after the separation—and five years before the divorce. It does support the notion that Barbara had unwittingly yoked herself to an institution rather than a person. That institution was a sort of extension of Robert Clifford's overwhelming need to invent, make and do in a nautical setting—and it was an exhausting institution. If you can't beat them, join them. In the end, that institution would morph into the modern Incat—the transformer of world fast sea transport. In the meantime, Barb brought up the children, and the children grew up as members of the extended Incat family, and the whole enterprise worked in the way that typical artisan/manufacturing families (like the jewellery-making Cliffords) worked in eighteenth and nineteenth century England, with the manufactory at the heart and all the extended family, business partners, tradesmen, apprentices clustered around.

Crucially, the manager of the Sandy Bay Branch of the ANZ Bank, Tony Travers, exercised his judgement to back the new SCFC business. In the old days, bank managers like Travers used their local knowledge of people, talent, track record and local economic circumstances to make informed investment-related decisions. That was how they added value; that was how Tony Travers, a proper banker, played his crucial part in the creation of Incat. A full generation later in 2003, a new generation of bankers (in a different bank), relying on crude centralised formulae rather than local human judgement, threw the mature Incat into a totally unnecessary and expensive receivership for nine months. But that is another story, for later on—about the dumbing down of banks and bankers.

From the start, the Sullivan's Cove Ferry Company business concept worked. The morning and evening ferry service turned a modest profit, but the real business lay in the recreational market— the lunchtime cruises for local business people, the weekend charters and so on. For the culinary side of things, all ex-fishermen know where to find the very best seafood (Barbara's curried scallops on rice were famous), and the Cliffords had had the wisdom to apply for a liquor licence to support the cruising. To their pleasant surprise, it turned out to be a licence to sell alcohol from 10.00 am to 10.00 pm. The first regular lunchtime cruise left the city centre wharf at 1.10 pm and returned promptly at 1.50 pm—by which time a barrel of beer had been consumed. A number of major local firms regularly decamped to the ferry for their lunchtimes.

This became the norm. At the height of the service, SCFC was running five lunchtime cruises per day. So a second boat was required, launched in 1973 by a very young Kim Clifford and named *James McCabe*—after another famous bushranger (for the record, both Matthew Brady and James McCabe were hanged in 1826). Robert Clifford was already trying to make an economical ferry boat go faster by good design, but he was hampered by materials. *James McCabe* was quite quick but just too heavy to go fast. All these early ships were spatchcocked together in bits—the Brady wheelhouse was actually constructed (like his first yacht in 1957) on the front lawn of the family home. She was a sturdy boat and is still shuttling tourists around the Sydney Harbour Bridge.

The Clifford learning curve during the leisure cruise period had less to do with ship-building technique and materials science (that came later) than with customer service. The years of fishing had taught Robert Clifford about servicing supply chains and about continuous technical innovation. Now he was learning to provide the customer with a stylish *experience* (not just a slice of transportation) and the company was edging into a *shuttle* kind of service—where the customer, not the provider, calls the shots at their convenience. The cruises were great fun and you could join one almost any time you wanted to. More to the point, SCFC fortuitously had a reserve of 16 staff in place on the night of Sunday, 5 January 1975.

Just a few days before that fateful night, Robert was driving home after a new year's party with old boyhood and lifelong friend 'Fuggle'—Peter Fuglsang. The latter remembers the conversation well (and Vivian Fuglsang, who was sitting in the back of the car, confirms it)—Fuglsang: 'What are you going to do next year?' Clifford: 'Somebody needs to knock the bridge down!'

PART TWO

Opportunity

The hero saves Hobart and
becomes a proper inventor

12

'Christ! I can see the casino!'

The earth moved for Ron Males at about 9.27 pm on Sunday night, 5 January 1975. About five seconds later, the crashing, grinding, roaring sound of a small earthquake reached the Males' family home in the riverside suburb of Lindisfarne, just over a mile from the Derwent Bridge. Ron's son Jonathan (later the international canoeist and Olympic coach), then 12 years of age, remembers his father's imperishable words vividly—because his father really wasn't a great swearer: 'Christ! I can see the casino!' You weren't supposed to be able to see the casino from the Males household because the bridge was in the line of sight—at least it had been until a few moments before.

Males senior had felt, then heard, then seen the result of the 7274-tonne bulk carrier MV *Lake Illawarra*, laden with 10 000 tonnes of zinc concentrate, ploughing through piers 18 and 19 of the bridge and bringing down 128 metres of four-lane concrete decking on itself. The ship is still 35 metres down at the bottom of the Derwent, along with most of the concrete. Seven of the crew were killed, plus five motorists unlucky enough to be crossing the bridge on a pleasant Sunday evening. (Even now, VIP visitors to

Hobart or new clients are sometimes offered a special treat by Robert Clifford—a trip over the sunken vessel with the sonar-imaging sounder turned on—the image of the ship is remarkably detailed and, of course, spooky.)

Robert Clifford was at a party that night and not having a lot of fun, so he decided to go down to the ferry terminal to lock up a boat that had been under repair. He was surprised to find a police roadblock around the docks. The policeman on duty waved him through: 'It's all right, Mr Clifford, you can go in.' He was still none the wiser, then he found his 'office' (a watchman's box) occupied by a well-known Hobart antiques dealer yelling into the phone, trying to get a rescue mounted. Clifford: 'What's going on?' The reply was: 'The bridge is down, cock!' Clifford: 'Don't be so bloody stupid—get off my phone!'

But he was right—that was why one of the boats was missing— one of the Sullivan's Cove Ferry Company's captains, Michael Grimwood, had already set off to lend a hand. Robert promptly followed. The Marine Board and Harbour Master were paralysed by indecision but Clifford knew roughly what to do. Why? Because 'I had fantasised about it happening'! One of his first errant thoughts was that this was the first bit of government assistance the fledgling firm had ever received (the *Lake Illawarra* was a government-owned ship).

13

'Strategic scenarios'— guessing the future

Within the hour, the Sullivan's Cove Ferry Company team had a ferry service up and running; by 2.00 am on Monday, Clifford was trying to organise a pile-driver to create new jetties. He was mentally prepared for the disaster and hence able to be decisive when the time came. In the business world, much play is made with 'scenario-scanning'—the practice of pre-living a range of possible futures—so as to be better prepared for whichever one turns up in real life. The method was developed originally by the big oil companies. In his own fashion, Clifford had scanned the bridge collapse 'scenario' and formulated a response to it. Peter Fuglsang suspects he *willed* it. Effectively, he took charge of Hobart's communications. All 16 of his staff turned up ready to lend a hand. He sent them home with instructions for the morning, by which time the SCFC had reverted to its roots as a ferry service; they were back in the transportation business.

There was the small matter of collecting the fares of the thousands of commuters now dependent on their two boats, the *Matthew Brady* (capacity 250 passengers, later extended to 310) and the *James McCabe* (capacity 150 passengers). SCFC was a commercial enterprise suddenly presented with a technical challenge and a business opportunity. So the SCFC team simply instituted a continuous fare-free service, confident that the government would recompense the firm in due course (they did). After three days of exhausting non-stop work, the government's Transport Commissioner telephoned Robert Clifford in the evening to thank the company for what they had done to rescue Hobart's communications system and to announce that from midnight they were authorised to charge fares of 20 cents, 10 cents and 5 cents (the normal river crossing ticket cost 25 cents).

After three sleepless days, Clifford's reaction was predictable enough. In the emergency, he had access to the dock phone only every 40 minutes. On the next arrival, he called the media to inform them that the service would cease at midnight and that message was delivered to the Transport Commissioner 40 minutes later. Another 40 minutes passed before a smiling Tasmanian Premier, Eric Reece, arrived on the wharf to announce: 'You charge whatever you like!' It was a bit of Clifford brinkmanship which instantly entered Hobart folklore.

There were still logistical problems, due mainly to the fact that there was simply no mechanism in place for ticketing thousands of customers. They were reduced to passing around a big rubbish bin, counting out the proceeds in the wheelhouse at day's end and then lugging buckets full of coins around to the Sandy Bay branch of the Australia and New Zealand Bank. The sitting room in the Clifford home was usually packed with bins full of coins waiting to be lugged to the bank. The manager Tony Travers' prescience in investing in SCFC was paying off. When the bridge came down, Barbara Clifford (Robert's ex-wife) was poised to start up a new career offshore, but found herself roped in to organise the office, the rosters and, of course, the alcohol. SCFC still had the liquor licence and the citizens of Hobart had had a nasty shock: they were surely entitled to a calming drop of beer during their daily commute. By the end of the first week, they were in full swing, carrying an extraordinary 26 000 passengers in the seven days following the bridge collapse.

The Cliffords understood from the start that Hobart had a big problem that wasn't going to go away quickly. Even in government circles, some innocent people were wondering if it might take a week or so to put things right. In fact, a temporary Bailey Bridge was finally thrown over the Derwent upstream nearly a year later, in December 1975. Until then, getting by car to the city from the eastern suburbs meant a 50 kilometre drive around the estuary. The age of the humble ferry had returned with a vengeance. The government's approach was to construct, at great cost, the infrastructure to support large 600–700 passenger ferries imported from other states and from overseas. Their mindset was of scheduled services, with the government provider calling the shots. The Cliffords had already learned the importance of convenience for the travelling public via the cruises. By the time they got a fourth ferry in service in mid-1975, they had a shuttle service of nimble smaller craft leaving every six minutes.

And, when trade for the government boats began to tail off later in the evening, the SCFC boats were still leaving full. Why? Because a trip with the Cliffords was always an experience and, of course, they still had the liquor licence. It's well known that Australians like a drink or three. At its height, the SCFC fleet actually became the largest licensee in Australia. On average, 126 eighteen-gallon barrels were tapped every week—the equivalent of 12 000 bottles of beer. As a business incubator, the firm was stimulating serious 'upstream' business at the state's breweries. As Robert Clifford puts it: 'For three years, I had the biggest hotel in Australia!' It was, in fact, the publican's dream—a reliable source of captive and thirsty customers that you 'get to kick out in twenty minutes time!' It seems appropriate somehow that the SCFC boats were known affectionately as 'the bushranger fleet'.

It took nearly three years to repair the bridge. The good people of Hobart had survived a terrible shock, they had adapted ingeniously to a new circumstance, and they had queued (mostly) in an orderly fashion to join the ferry service (although one Deputy Premier of Tasmania was thrown off the ferry for queue-jumping by an irate fellow passenger). Photographs of the mile-long, snaking lines of congenial passengers are a poignant reminder of an intensely lived period. Marriages—and of course various liaisons—were made and broken by the disruption to ordinary life, regular travelling 'clubs' were formed, one person died on board and two went missing completely.

For the uninitiated, Hobart, though technically a 'capital' city (of the State of Tasmania) is generally a sleepy kind of place. There is a grand State Parliament building and even a grandee in uniform as the Queen's man in Tasmania—the Governor—all for a state of fewer than half a million people. At that time, Hobart's population was well under 200 000 people. So the collapse of the bridge—the city's 'choke point'—livened things up considerably. Over the next three years, SCFC supplied nine million passenger journeys and Robert Clifford—the city's saviour—lodged in the minds of Tasmanians as a larger-than-life swashbuckling figure.

14

The family moves on

The Clifford family lived intensively too. Young Craig and Kim (aged seven and five when the bridge went down) were beginning to realise how important their father was (reminiscent, in a way, of the young Robert's discovery that strange men would cross the road to avoid confrontation with his starting-price bookie father), and they regarded it as perfectly normal to be picked up from school by any one of the SCFC crew and to spend hours on the ferries. Both of the kids were on board on one occasion when Fred succeeded in running the *James McCabe* into the Sullivan's Cove wharf, accompanied by a screaming son on shore (this was obviously after Robert had taken over the dominant role in their regular screaming matches).

The children were learning to be self-sufficient but also to understand the role of sound organisation in the running of life. Their mother actually had matching different-coloured tracksuits for them for each day of the week. Everybody was always very busy. Craig, of course, was required to sail competitively—everybody who is anybody in Hobart sails, and many in regular competition. It is revealing that Craig called his Sabot-class yacht *Keep Calm* in recognition of his father's constant screamed advice from the rescue boat. Evenings were spent in hoarse reconstruction of the race, leg by leg. Craig's grandfather Fred never knew his own father but everybody understood that the Fred–Robert screaming matches were a perfectly normal way (for them) to solve practical problems on the hoof and to express affection. So it seemed perfectly reasonable to Robert Clifford to raise his own son the same way. Kim, being a girl, was allowed to be a recreational sailor, but her Sundays were still spent at the Derwent Sailing Squadron.

Craig was now old enough to grasp that he and his father, united in mutual affection, operated on different mental planets. Craig was always more philosophical in outlook and, most people agreed, broader and less single-minded. Thus, his contribution to the family business, assuming it arose at all, was bound to be complementary to that of his extraordinary father. He remembers one typical day at the Sailing Squadron:

It was a lunchtime, and I had been racing in the morning. Still in my wetsuit, I sat in the car on a towel while RFC gave me the run-down on all the things I had done wrong in the morning races (as you could imagine, little time was spent on what I may have done right!). It was time to get back on the water so I opened the car door to get out, but RFC had not finished the debrief and continued talking. I closed the car door again and turned to listen. RFC questioned why I had closed the door, to which I shrugged and replied: 'What's the problem, why does it matter?' RFC's reply to me was: 'That's one less time that door will work!' I remember being bewildered by this response, recognising at the time that the way his mind and my mind worked were on occasion not going to align. That recognition continues today; not right, not wrong, just different. (correspondence, 2009)

The story illustrates not just the exigencies of father–son communication, it also exposes Robert Clifford's almost obsessional attention to detail, to efficiency of operation and to the elimination of waste.

15

The real turning point

Many people in Australia take the view that the bridge collapse, and the revenue stream it created for SCFC, actually caused the later Incat phenomenon. The truth is that it did provide seedcorn money for further developments—and it also bankrolled Fred's entry into the world of owning and training racing 'trotters'—but it wasn't the crucial turning point in this history. That came from the lease of the British-built 64-passenger hovercraft renamed *Michael Howe* (another bushranger, of course, who escaped custody in 1817 and was killed on the run the following year). In the scramble for ferries after the disaster, all kinds of craft found their way to Hobart—some of them unseaworthy or otherwise unsuitable for the task.

The *Michael Howe* is important because it got Robert Clifford thinking hard again about the principles of ship design. Forget the swashbuckling, forget the money-making, Clifford is fundamentally an inventor with a truly scientific mind, impelled to understand how and why things work—or don't work in the case of the *Michael Howe*. It was a Jekyll and Hyde sort of craft. The Jekyll was a very comfortable ship twice as fast as the conventional ferries and much loved for its stylishness by the customers—so much so that SCFC could charge double price for the tickets. The Hyde was an eccentric, poorly designed craft that swallowed up about 75 per cent of the total maintenance bill of the ferry fleet. Like many British inventions, it was clever, quirky and impractical. At the time, Robert Clifford went on record: 'If the British can sell 34 heaps of rubbish like this [around the world], how many properly engineered fast ships could we sell from Tasmania?'

The challenge for Clifford was to figure out how to preserve its virtues while eliminating its deficiencies. It was, as Clifford observed, 'a cat with a skirt!'; that is, a craft with the excellent load-carrying capacity of a catamaran, allied to a virtually frictionless ride. But its shape was clumsily high and square and its propulsion, by high-speed diesel via small belt-driven propellers through an inefficient 'vee' gearbox, was wasteful. The trick would be to take the principle of the catamaran down a different path. Cats have certain advantages over monohulls—they require less power for a given speed and the available deck space is ideal for carrying passengers. So Clifford reasoned that if you could make a cat big and stable enough to transport vehicles over oceans, and you could make it light, it would go very fast and thus transform a large chunk of sea travel.

In the meantime, they built two more 'bushranger' ferries in record time to service the new commuter traffic: the *Martin Cash* and the *Lawrence Kavanagh*. These were conventional steel monohulls, and, because they were effectively to enter government service, they had to be certified as seaworthy. This was the Cliffords' first brush with formal design process and proper naval architecture. The new ships did their bit over the next two years while the new bridge was being built, but it was clear that the heavy-duty ferry business would be wiped out soon. So, in 1977, the Sullivan's Cove Ferry Company was gradually wound down to be replaced the following year by the grandly named International Catamarans Pty Ltd, controlled jointly by Robert Clifford (as designer/boat-builder) and the incoming Philip Hercus (as naval architect/designer). By then, they had nailed their colours to the mast as designers and builders of fast catamarans. The firm's first employee was Kerry Sturmey—the new romantic love in Robert's life and already hard at work in the business.

The new firm represented Robert Clifford's final commitment to ship-building as a life's work and he was not yet 35 years of age. Everything else—the fishing, the ferrying, the printing, even the flirtation with ocean yacht racing—has to be seen as ancillary to the main game. Since the age of three or four, Clifford had been a creative person who needed to be making and doing—for whom any other calling would be second best and a probable source of unhappiness and failure. Some people are like this; they need a vocation or, more correctly, their vocation is revealed to them at a young age—if they are lucky. Pilots in aviation tend to know by the age of 10 that that is what it has to be. James Dyson, the multimillionaire inventor–entrepreneur who brought us the revolutionary bagless vacuum cleaner, was always like this.

In hindsight, it wasn't obvious in 1978 that the traditional ship-building world needed a new manufacturer devoted exclusively to fast catamarans, but it was clear that Robert Clifford needed to be in the designing, making and doing business. At that time, Clifford—the visionary—was a lone voice in the shipping world in *knowing* that catamaran design represented the way forward for fast sea transport. Thirty years later, in 2007, there were 66 fast ferries under construction all over the world: of these, just two were monohulls, one was a hovercraft and one a hydrofoil; the other 62 were cats.

Back in 1978, Clifford had already figured out that, with a couple of very slim hulls and with all the hovercraft airlift equipment removed, you could make a boat with more frictional resistance than a hovercraft but much improved wave-making resistance—a trade-off. The hovercraft obviously had little frictional resistance (that was its party trick) but awful wave-making resistance—it actually depressed the water under the craft. He calculated they could double the speed of their ferries from 9 to 18 knots. He started by building a model (of course) but the shipping authorities had decreed that no novel design would be approved without the supervision of a proper naval architect—and there weren't many in Tasmania. That is how Robert ended up in Sydney plonking his model on the desk of Philip Hercus with a request to improve on it. After some tank testing and a lot of calculation, Hercus rang Robert to report: 'We're going to get 26 knots!' By then he was hooked; it was the beginning of a very fruitful 10-year business partnership.

And they did get 26 knots. At their first try, they succeeded in building a very fast catamaran (the *Jeremiah Ryan*) capable of carrying nearly 150 passengers and crew—nearly three times the payload of the *Michael Howe*. What's more, because she was a catamaran her 7.7 metre beam meant she could accommodate wide, comfortable seats and plenty of walking-around space. And because they had built the accommodation unit separately from the hulls, cabin noise and vibration were minimal. She was not only fast, she was comfortable. *Jeremiah Ryan* was actually built in a government-owned 'wharf shed' at Prince of Wales Bay by a rag-bag of contracted 'expert' tradesmen, all of whom were maritime industry friends of the Cliffords. This was the beginning of a loose association of boat-builders with multifarious business and social connections, including sailing together at the weekend.

Jeremiah Ryan was a good start on the way to a fast and comfortable cat, but it had two principal disadvantages. The hull was made of steel so it was too heavy to go *really* fast, and it didn't *look* fast—in fact it looked like an ugly duckling. They had planned an all-aluminium superstructure but couldn't get their hands on enough alloy, so it was part aluminium and part lightweight timber. That boat, launched by Robert's mother Eve, is listed as 'hull 001' in the Incat hall of fame (at the time of writing, the 112-metre hull 066 has recently entered service on the Dover–Boulogne run over the English Channel). *Jeremiah Ryan*, still fast, still ugly, is still trading on the river as the *Derwent Explorer* 35 years later so, despite its looks, it is a very *sound* boat.

16

'Weight is a state of mind!'

The first boat actually sold by International Catamarans was the *James Kelly* (hull 002), built in 1979. It looked a bit better than *Jeremiah Ryan*, although not yet exactly sexy. It was faster and smaller than *Jeremiah Ryan* and it brought in a bit of money during a lean start-up period for the new firm. Its real importance is that the superstructure (but not yet the hull) was constructed entirely of lightweight aluminium. A useful by-product of that, maintained in all succeeding designs, was the consequent separation of hull from superstructure—just like *Jeremiah Ryan*—thus reducing vibration.

Clifford had always known that weight would be the determinant of efficiency in the future and that aluminium, although a difficult material to fabricate, brought with it substantial benefits—another trade-off. If you begin your aquatic career in dinghy racing, you are going to understand the importance of weight—a subject about which Robert Clifford is famously obsessive. It seems to have been almost physically painful for Clifford to agree to the installation of heavy escalators and lifts in the 112-metre fast ferries built for service between the islands of Japan (hulls 064 and 065), but the customer is always right.

The years 1977–1979 were the 'wilderness years' for the nascent Incat (technically still International Catamarans Pty Ltd at this stage) because nobody wanted to buy their fast ugly ducklings. They kept their heads above water—just. So the order for a 20-metre all-aluminium fast ferry for the Barrier Reef tourist trade was the breakthrough they needed. Clifford and Hercus got the design for *Fitzroy* (hull 004) right from the start. They had built in a cost margin for the complication of aluminium, so when it turned out to be cheaper to manufacture than steel it became very profitable. 'We had overcome our fear of the unknown and built an excellent aluminium vessel at our first try.'

On the delivery voyage of the *Fitzroy*, Incat picked up a further five orders for similar vessels by the simple expedient of stopping overnight at the various resort islands on the route from Hobart to Cairns. One prospective buyer even sent a pre-contract cheque for the entire boat in advance, so keen was he to get his hands on the new vessel. *Fitzroy* was irresistible to the island owners and operators because she looked so good—stylishly fast. She was also capable of carrying 200 people the 65–80 kilometres to the outer Barrier Reef at an operating speed of 24 knots. This transformed the business of the ferry operators as they could squeeze in more trips every week. Clifford had been a ferryman and he understood the ferryman's problems and mind-set. This is yet another lesson from the business school world that Robert Clifford did not need to be taught by a professor: if you succeed in getting inside the mind of your customer, you will always drive away competitors who can't see beyond this year's bottom line.

From then on they were set fair. There was a market for very fast and good-looking catamarans, and it turned out you could build a sturdy ship in aluminium relatively cheaply and hence profitably. What's more, the speed, carrying capacity and quick turn-around time of InCat's ships actually transformed the nature of the Barrier Reef tourist trade. Before the fast cats came along, only dedicated enthusiasts could visit the reef on slow fishing-type vessels. Over the next 15 years, seven Incat-designed vessels brought a multimillion dollar international tourist business to the Port Douglas area.

As they say: 'If you build a better mousetrap, the world will beat a path to your door.' What's more, a better ship exports value—initially to the operator and his customers—but in the long run to the environment as well. Robert Clifford did not set out with the aim of building an ecologically sound craft with a tiny carbon footprint; he just wanted to build a better, more efficient ship. But if you achieve that, not only will the world beat a path to your door, you will automatically achieve a greater quantum of transportation while using less fuel. (They do say that the best things in life—like love, happiness, virtue, wealth and so on—are always by-products of some higher pursuit. If you go after them directly, you destroy them. Build a better ship; you get a better carbon footprint, and so, in ship-building terms, you achieve virtue.)

So the next few years were a time of growth and consolidation for Incat. They continued to build a variety of ships—a fast utility boat to support dam construction; an all-aluminium ocean-racing yacht (the *Margaret Rintoul IV*); a first freight-carrying cat; and a 22-metre fast cat with novel surface-piercing propellers—all in the interests of experiment and learning. But the core business remained the continuous improvement of the fast cats. In 1982, they sold 10 ships, some of them built under licence, including China's first all-aluminium vessel.

The utility boat, named *Trojan*, provided an early opportunity to cock a snook at the authorities (already a Clifford speciality) and get some local publicity. The Tasmanian Government was forced by a groundswell of public opinion to call a halt to the construction of the Gordon below Franklin dam on environmental grounds. This obliged them to compensate all the disadvantaged contractors on the dam project. As *Trojan* was now out of work, Clifford shifted her to Constitution Dock in the heart of Hobart and decked her out in large black signwriting: 'Unemployed South West Contractor'.

It achieved nothing in terms of compensation, but it succeeded in keeping the firm and its works on centre stage.

In all, 80 vessels were constructed under licence in boatyards in the United States, the United Kingdom, Hong Kong and New Zealand. The Tasmanian Government by now realised it had a business incubator in its midst and cleared the way for the firm to buy land at Sullivan's Cove for expansion. At long last Incat would be able to build ships in their own premises. *Keppel Cat 1*, launched in September 1984, was actually the first Incat ship to be built on a site owned by the company. The State Government also helped to lobby the Federal Government for development funding. The bushrangers were getting respectable.

17

Getting into bed with James Sherwood

By 1985, they were building two 30-metre, 30-knot fast cats (*Our Lady Patricia* and *Our Lady Pamela*) for James Sherwood's Sea Containers Ltd in London. They were destined for the Portsmouth to Ryde service over the Solent in southern England. *Patricia* was launched in November 1985 and despatched to Antwerp on a bulk carrier. When the heavy-lift crane deposited her in Belgian waters, the new English crew thought they were in for a three-day jolly to Portsmouth. They got there in a day. The *Patricia* delivery was also the 16-year-old Kim Clifford's first overseas visit—flying with the crew in economy class while her father upgraded. This was an early exposure to the realities of corporate status for a budding Incat director who absolutely needed to understand the human element from top to bottom. When the time came to deliver the sister ship *Pamela*, there was no suitable bulk carrier on the Tasmanian side of Singapore so they did the obvious—sailed the ship all the way to Portsmouth. It took them 41 days to unite the two sisters. The DIY delivery saved them three weeks and about A$100 000.

The two ladies (*Patricia* and *Pamela*) are an important part of the tale for two reasons. Firstly, *Pamela* set the pattern for worldwide fast ferry operations: the ability of these ships to migrate quickly, usually seasonally, to wherever the business is. Like the ski instructors who chase snow around the world, the big fast cat can get to anywhere quite quickly and get to work immediately. Later on, this turned out to be a big selling point to the military. *Our Lady Pamela* is still at work on the 4.5-mile Isle of Wight passage, having (in 2008) completed 160 000 crossings and transported some 13 million people (the equivalent of about 30 times around the equator). *Our Lady Patricia* eventually became the first Incat craft to be scrapped (in 2007), but her cannibalised spares help to keep her sister ship going.

The other key event at this time was the new business relationship with James Sherwood, the ebullient chief executive of Sea Containers Ltd. Sherwood struck many people as the same kind of swashbuckler as Robert Clifford. He was 10 years older than Clifford but both were highly entrepreneurial, combative and successful risk-takers and they worked remarkably well together—until it all ended in tears. Sherwood had started out as a cargo officer in the US Navy, so he knew plenty about sea transportation and he was clever enough to see the container revolution coming. He was a Yale-educated American turned Anglophile. At about the time Robert Clifford started buying antique Rolls-Royce cars, Sherwood was buying the equally antique *Illustrated London News* and publishing his quirky restaurant and hotel guidebook *James Sherwood's Discriminating Guide to London*. Sea Containers has always been based in the tax haven of Bermuda but its iconic headquarters is perched on the south bank of the Thames in central London.

The big difference between the two men was in the matter of business focus. Sherwood had always been (in business parlance) a 'bottom-feeder': a man who would seize upon any business at all that looked like it might turn a dollar or two. His company, from its Bermuda base, consistently reconfigured itself to stay ahead of US tax law. Incat, always based in Hobart, was in the fast cat business and little else. There were the associated Incat licensing deals, charter partnerships, property holdings and design boutiques, but all in the service of building a better ship. Meanwhile, Sherwood took Sea Containers from its hugely successful core business in container leasing into luxury hotels, railroads, plantations, property and many other interests. His connection with Clifford arose from his purchase of a couple of British ferry operations and, indirectly, his ownership of the Venice–Simplon Orient Express. Over the next few years, Sherwood and Clifford achieved a remarkable business synergy.

18

Piercing waves

This is a story punctuated by dramatic breakthroughs, some of them essentially technical or scientific. So far, the story is of a weight-obsessed scientist/inventor pushing the boundaries of ship design and manufacture. The rethinking of the hovercraft logic was important and so was the introduction of lightweight construction using metal alloys. But Clifford could see already, as the ships got bigger to serve different markets, they were beginning to bump into new problems inherent in fast cat design. In the end, he could see they would need to be able to carry big loads (cars and trucks) over longer distances, which means over rough ocean seas. He had not (yet) foreseen a demand for very big and very fast military vessels to transport heavy matériel to battle zones all around the world—that came later.

It's not clear whether the original wave-piercing idea arose from watching a film of the 20-metre *Tangalooma* (hull 005, launched in 1981) slicing at full speed through rough (2-metre) seas on its way to a New Year's Eve party, or from the uncomfortable experience of riding in rough weather on *Quicksilver* (hull 008, launched in 1982), but the idea began to emerge of a smarter way to propel a fast catamaran in big seas—not bouncing over the waves but slicing through them. It's all very well to build a faster ferry, but if the ride is uncomfortable it defeats the object. So the seat-of-the pants hunch about 'wave-piercing' (remember Howard Gardner and the location of the bodily-kinaesthetic intelligence?) arose in action and in observation—not from theoretical textbooks.

So it was back to the drawing board—and the model making. This time, Incat had the clout to secure some government support for taking the wave-piercing idea forward. The cover photograph shows the 40-year-old Robert Clifford looking like a somewhat sensitive Viking warrior and holding one of the many wave-piercer models—much more like an inventor than a businessman. By the end of 1983, with James Sherwood already on the scene, after the usual long trail of smaller prototypes, they were able to launch a serious 8-metre prototype wave-piercer—the *Little Devil* (hull 013). It carried only six people perched on top of a kind of double outrigger and was powered only by a 20-horsepower longshaft outboard motor. The prototype immediately began to demonstrate its prowess in disturbed water, but it was still a very new idea in marine technology.

The wave-piercing concept represented, in fact, an ingenious compromise between the simplicity of a conventional catamaran and the sophistication of the SWATH (small waterplane area twin hull) concept which placed the craft on very skinny struts connected to (effectively) a couple of underwater torpedoes or submarines. SWATH vessels are very good at reducing motion in rough seas (because much of the buoyancy rides calmly beneath the waves), rather like transferring the smoothness of a submarine's motion to the experience of seafarers above the surface. But they have disadvantages, too, such as a very deep draught and the need for short length overall. Good design always represents an intelligent compromise with physics—that is, with nature—and it tends to evolve by trial and error over time. So this was a new compromise with the forces of nature.

Yet in just *six years* from the launch of the primitive *Little Devil*, Robert Clifford and James Sherwood would be quaffing champagne while standing on the deck of a 74.9-metre wave-piercing catamaran ferry close to Bishop Rock lighthouse at the edge of the Atlantic Ocean, celebrating the fastest ocean crossing ever by a passenger ship. (It was a 'dry' ship but somebody had had the presence of mind to stash away a bottle of bubbly.) Incat would thus come to possess the famous Hales Trophy—the 'Blue Riband'—for the achievement of the fastest Atlantic crossing—in a vessel essentially based on that 8-metre prototype. It is no exaggeration to say that this is one of the most remarkable concept-to-fulfilment achievements in the history of technology development. As Dick Smith asks: 'How did he do it?'

Those six years were a time of dramatic technological development. Following the *Little Devil* prototype, in June 1985, they built the first proper wave-piercer, the 28-metre *Spirit of Victoria*. It was only a moderate success commercially, but it taught them a lot about the wave-piercing concept. It sat high (too high) in the water, looking a bit like a hydrofoil. Philip Hercus was now in the background keeping them honest as to the nautical rules and regulations—you had to have the buoyancy somewhere, but *Spirit of Victoria* just had too much in the twin hulls. By the time they built *Tassie Devil 2001* the following year, they had worked out that you could transfer reserve buoyancy to the forward central hull. This meant that the prow of the ship didn't get wet at all until you encountered medium-sized waves, then it did its job in keeping the nose of the craft afloat by adding dynamic lift when the bow encountered a wave. Meanwhile, the two main hulls could get on with their job of slicing straight through the waves while providing the main buoyancy. In the calm, it was a cat; in rough seas, it became a sort of part-time trimaran.

But the Incat team had not solved all the problems. They sailed *Tassie Devil 2001* to Fremantle in Western Australia to serve as one of the support boats for the America's Cup yachting contest in February

1987. Once she got there she was the talk of Fremantle—she looked terrific and her speed, comfort and economy outshone all the competitive boats. But on the way across the Great Australian Bight, her skittish side showed through. It was an exciting voyage in a big following sea; so much so that they were actually surfing down the face of the big waves that roll up from the Antarctic—the sort of thing any yachtsperson loves. Unfortunately, one of the waves was a bit too big—as they surfed down at about 35 knots, the foredeck tripped the crest of the wave and the resulting avalanche of water smashed a forward-facing window.

Robert Clifford has an interesting scar on his forehead. When the water came in, he had been sitting a couple of rows back in the main cabin—just behind the bar—which, uprooted by the huge rush of water, and complete with its refrigerators, deposited itself on his head. The ship was fine—catamarans have enormous reserves of buoyancy in their watertight hulls—but the electronics engineer did decide it would be prudent to do some bailing out before attending to the severely concussed skipper. Afterwards, he needed 26 stitches in that forehead. As Clifford points out, plenty of sailors end an evening's drinking hitting their heads on the bar; very few can lay claim to assault by the bar. Another Clifford first.

This would not be the last time that an exciting accident accelerated the technical development process (the next occasions, in 1990 and 1994, were to be much more spectacular—and public). But the story does demonstrate the limitations of tank testing and computer modelling. Incat, in comparison with most of its competitors, has always tested its prototype designs in the real world of water and weather. It is only *in extremis* that you find out the limitations of any design. (At about the same time, Qantas, the Australian airline, was installing standard operating procedures to ensure that its pilots spent a substantial proportion of their time actually flying the aircraft, rather than over-relying on the automatic pilot and 'fly-by-wire' technology as other airlines sometimes did. In aviation, as in sailing, the *feel* of things is crucial for safety when things get tricky.)

There is nothing anti-intellectual about this insistence on the seat-of-the-pants feel of complex systems in operation in the real world. The feel of things actually complements the calculations and the simulations. This is the sort of thing Robert Clifford, the modeller and inventor, had been doing since he was 14. It may explain the technical and operational superiority of the Incat fleet.

James Sherwood, as usual, was active in the background. The decision to go ahead with construction of a big wave-piercing car-carrying ferry for Sea Containers was made when Clifford and Sherwood met on board *Tassie Devil 2001* in Fremantle. They built two more fast cats before the Sea Containers order was taken up—a 31-metre companion vessel to *Tassie Devil 2001* (*2000*) and the 37-metre *Sea Flight* for a New Zealand charterer. *Sea Flight* was launched in November 1988 and endured a nightmare delivery voyage to Auckland, courtesy of a dementedly overconfident Kiwi skipper—a man who alternated wildly between ploughing at full speed into huge oncoming seas ('The ship is handling it well!') and panic ('Prepare to abandon ship if necessary!').

They got to Auckland, a bit shaken, after surviving an engine fire and the shipping of rather a lot of water. The fast ferry world tends to attract the swashbuckling type. The upside of that terrible voyage was that it taught them, once again, something about the potential and limitations of the craft in extreme conditions. As a result of the rough treatment, *Sea Flight* helped to solve the buoyancy problem: they had finally got enough buoyancy into the central hull to ensure that no more bars would be uprooted and dumped on passengers. And the two new ships were bigger—carrying 390 and 350 people respectively.

19

Learning from experience

Robert Clifford's story is essentially that of an inventor. To describe him only as an entrepreneur or as a businessman is technically correct but woefully inadequate. This is a person impelled to build models and to test (if need be to destruction) the utility of prototypes in the real world. Tank testing is the fallback of the naval designer but nothing supplants the 'seat-of-the-pants' *feel* of physics in action. The great yachting helmsmen find it as difficult to describe what they are doing right as the great dancers do. Perhaps only an artist of the highest rank can describe what is involved because there is certainly no mathematical formula or technique.

Nobel Prize-winner William Golding, in his novel *Rites of Passage* (1980), gets nearest to capturing the sailing experience. His nineteenth-century hero, Edmund Talbot, is a few days into a sailing ship passage to Australia. He has not sailed before and this is an old and uncomfortable tub. In his journal, Talbot describes his first storm at sea in the Bay of Biscay. He has been heartily seasick and has ventured up on deck just after dark and at the height of a storm:

For some reason, though the water stung my face it put me in a good humour. Philosophy and religion—what are they when the wind blows and the water gets up in lumps? I stood there, holding on with one hand, and began positively to enjoy all this confusion, lit as it was by the last lees of light. Our huge old ship with her few and shortened sails from which the rain cascaded was beating into this sea and therefore shouldering the waves at an angle, like a bully forcing his way through a dense crowd. And as the bully might encounter here and there a like spirit, so she (our ship) was hindered now and then, or dropped or lifted or, it may be, struck a blow in the face that made all her forepart, then the waist and the afterdeck, to foam and wash with white water. I began, as Wheeler had put it, to ride a ship. Her masts leaned a little. The shrouds to windward were taut, those to leeward slack, or very near it. The huge cable of her mainbrace swung out to leeward between the masts; and now here is a point which I would wish to make. Comprehension of this vast engine is not to be come at gradually nor by poring over diagrams in Marine Dictionaries! It comes, when it comes, at a bound. In that semi-darkness between one wave and the next I found the ship and the sea comprehensible not merely in terms of her mechanical ingenuity but as a—a what? As a steed, a conveyance, a means of working to an end. This was a pleasure I had not anticipated. It was, I thought with perhaps a touch of complacency, quite an addition to my understanding! (p. 16)

This is as good a description you could hope for of how intuition, or perhaps revelation, works. Robert Clifford the sailor succeeded, and sometimes failed, because of his deep trust in this human faculty. Tank testing and mathematics are necessary, but never sufficient.

PART THREE
Establishment

Anatomy of a new business

20

Turning points

The entire history of Robert Clifford and Incat seems to be punctuated by turning points; nothing, it seems, was determined from the start—except possibly for the gifted capacity of the infant Clifford. Yet, even if we leave aside the family structure—birth order, the tempestuous relationship with his father Fred and so on—events unfolded in a seemingly deterministic way. The Meccano sets stimulated the making and doing genius, the translation to the middle-class school over the river, the years of ferry journeys, the 'crystallising moment' of skill at the helm of a yacht, the grounding apprenticeship in a small business, the years of adapting and inventing small boats for commercial fishing, the downfall of the Tasman bridge and the attendant customer-facing business opportunity, the inspiration about catamaran design and, perhaps most important, the commitment to ship-building as the vocational and professional goal in life. In simple terms, Robert Clifford spent his twenties fishing, his thirties running ferries (the latter half building them as well) and his forties establishing an international business and capturing about half of the world market for big and very fast ferries.

From the technical standpoint, the crucial turning point was the year 1989: it was an extraordinary leap from the 37-metre *Sea Flight* (hull 022), launched at the end of 1988, to the launch in January 1990 of the 74-metre *Christopher Columbus* (hull 025). In just over a year, they had not only doubled the length of the craft, they had shifted from propeller drive to water-jets, introduced the carriage of all cargoes, including vehicles, and increased the maximum lightship speed by 35 per cent (from 31 knots to 42 knots)—all at the same time (lightship speed here means the top speed of the vessel unladen with cargo, passengers, vehicles, water, etc.). Any one of those innovations might have proved beyond them but all of them worked—and in concert. And, as Gregory Bateson, the anthropologist and philosopher, reminds us on pp. 91–2, the doubling of length means *eight* times the volume. *Christopher Columbus* (soon to be renamed *Hoverspeed Great Britain*) was not only faster, she was much, much bigger. Incat had built its first big boat and it was also about to become a bigger company. And, in June of 1990, *Hoverspeed Great Britain* proved she could cross the Atlantic Ocean in 3 days, 7 hours and 52 minutes at an average speed of 36.97 knots.

This was the outcome of Clifford and Sherwood challenging for the Hales Trophy for the fastest crossing of the Atlantic. The famous 'Blue Riband' thus passed to *Hoverspeed Great Britain*. The Americans were grumpy, of course, regarding the 38-year reign of USS *United States* as a kind of birthright; so they claimed (until they read the Hales rules more carefully) that *Hoverspeed Great Britain* wasn't a proper passenger ship. In fact, she only held the Blue Riband for eight years. In 1998, Hull 047 (the Spanish *Catalonia*) raised the bar to 38.85 knots and just a month later hull 049 (the Danish *Cat-Link V*) irritated the Iberians (*Catalonia* was operated by the Spanish subsidiary of the Argentinian ferry company Buquebus, which was owned by a Uruguayan) by achieving an average of 41.284 knots. That was in July 1998 and, at the time of writing, the Danes still hold the trophy. Thus, by the end of the twentieth century, the most famous prize in shipping had been won by three successive vessels built in the same yard.

Robert Clifford was just 40 years of age in 1983 when he secured government funding to experiment with wave-piercing prototypes. When he stood on the deck of *Hoverspeed Great Britain* with James Sherwood and the Hales Trophy, he was 47. In those seven years, the Incat mission crystallised, in much the same way as the 13-year-old boy's sense of mission crystallised at the helm of an 11-foot dinghy some 30 years before. And the 40-something boat-builder was now having to grapple with great complexity (they do say in the business schools this is what marks out the successful leader—not the personality or the drive, that is taken for granted—but the ability to juggle a lot of balls and remain more or less sane). Scholars of giftedness in children stress that it manifests itself mainly in superior cognitive ability (Jacobsen, *The Gifted Adult*, 2000). Gifted people are somehow able to zoom in on what is important (and to 'park' what is not), to learn very quickly over a broad front and to keep a weather eye out for the long-term 'big picture'.

21

Things get complicated

As the firm began to grow, so the complexity began to mount. The first complication lay in the new relationship with government—both at the state and the federal level. Tasmania has always been a relatively poor state and, consequently, the State Government has historically sought to support any employer likely to grow a successful indigenous business. The government knew full well about Tasmania's proud 168-year tradition of successful ship-building (in 1853, Tasmania built no fewer than 118 vessels of 78-tonne average weight), supported after the Second World War by a generous ship-building 'bounty' to protect local builders from competition. In hindsight, it is easy to see how Incat was likely to become the nucleus of an industrial 'cluster' of supporting firms. Nowadays, it is the grandly titled 'Tasmanian Light Shipbuilding Cluster', and it has attracted the attention of grandees like Harvard's Professor Michael Porter (see p. 98), whose research into such 'clusters' around the world informed his famous book *The Competitive Advantage of Nations* (1990).

But it wasn't until Clifford started to sell a lot of boats in Queensland that the Tasmanian Government started to take an interest and to lobby the Federal Government on Incat's behalf—so the political complexities of the two governments became a factor. The A$6 million guarantee for experiments in wave-piercing was one initiative, but more practical still was the State Government's support for Incat to buy land at Sullivan's Cove in Hobart for expansion in 1982. Robert Clifford's long-term vision was for Tasmania taking charge of a new international fast ferry market—and for that he would need lots of space to build the ships. In 2002, when Incat went into receivership (that part of the tale is still to come), a State Labor Government got short shrift from a conservative administration in Canberra. But, back in 1982, the State Government had plans for a new Bass Strait crossing to Sydney, so Clifford's ideas about bigger and faster vessels were of direct interest to them.

•

At the same time, life was getting more complicated on the technology front. In 1984, Robert had made his first visit to the Boeing factory in Seattle, mainly to inspect the design of very large hangar doors—with a new covered shipyard in Hobart in mind. While he was there, he immersed himself in the way that Boeing was putting together its aircraft—essentially the riveting together of large sub-assemblies sent in from all over the world. Boeing's essential 'value add', he noted, was in knowing how to put it all together very quickly and securely. It could not have been more different from traditional ship-building, where you lay down a keel and work outwards sequentially from there.

In that same year, Robert Clifford bought his first (of many) vintage Rolls-Royces. That first Roller had been built in 1935 rather like a ship, with all the bits bolted onto a massive steel chassis. By that time, Henry Royce (a Clifford hero) was also looking for ways to use aluminium wherever possible in his cars, in search of lighter weight, but he was stuck with the chassis. The modern automobile is much lighter and quicker to manufacture because of its 'monocoque' construction; some expensive ones even have bodies constructed from aluminium. The great strength and durability come not from a massive steel backbone but from the monocoque structure itself—the whole is greater than the sum of the parts.

Courtesy of Robert Clifford, a new ship-building phrase 'sea frame' entered the language alongside 'air frame'—the term commonly used to describe the construction of the basic shell of a commercial aircraft. It is a kind of magic—strength without weight. For Clifford, lightness + power = speed—and speed, as he had proven on the outer Barrier Reef, transforms the businesses of the customers. From then on, Incat was a ship-builder in name only—they were morphing into a kind of nautical aircraft assembly operation, but employing the most tricky material of all—aluminium. And, as in the aircraft industry, they were constructing the basic shell and leaving the details to the customer. That first Clifford-owned Rolls-Royce had a body put together by H.J. Mulliner & Co. of Chiswick, London.

Ever since *Jeremiah Ryan* was built in 1977, Incat had understood that aluminium had to be the solution to the weight problem in a fast ship. Marine-grade aluminium is about one-third the weight of steel and normally incorporates about five to six per cent of other elements, including manganese and magnesium. The marine alloy has the additional advantage of high resistance to corrosion and denting, and is even non-sparking and non-magnetic—crucial in a minesweeper. The modern big (112-metre) cat carries about 950 tonnes of high-strength marine-grade aluminium alloy plates and extrusions and some of the sub-assemblies are as big as small houses. Part of the magic of aluminium is that, not only will it not rust, if it is left naked (unpainted) it will coat itself in an oxide once it is exposed to salt water. Commercial ferry operators like to paint their ships in fancy livery; the military, it turns out, are quite happy to save dollars and let nature take its course.

The metal is sourced in structural sections and the plate comes from specialised suppliers in Europe. In the 1990s, Rio Tinto Alcan in France, prompted by Incat, developed a specialised alloy called Sealium with much-improved strength and corrosion resistance as compared with the regular alloys used in ship-building. This is a persistent pattern—Incat driving suppliers to higher and higher standards in order to meet the specialised requirements of the fast cats. The aluminium sections are then purpose-cut in Hobart using Incat proprietary software. The trick lies in how you put it all together because aluminium is such a notoriously difficult material to work with—it is heat-sensitive to welding (unlike steel), it flexes, it sometimes shrinks and it actually *cries* when it is welded. Also, you have to keep the alloy scrupulously clean before you attempt to weld it. The new hero of the hour became the specialist welder armed with years of training and almost magical craft skills. Even the most skilled steel welders needed substantial retraining to master this new skill and some never made it at all. Sometimes trained carpenters turned out to be better new-start employees because they were much better than many steel welders at cutting, shaping and planing—the artistic aspects of craft work.

This is a long way removed from the modern auto-assembly plant where the 'skill' resides mainly in the robots—so much more reliable than any human being. In aircraft and automobile manufacture you can assemble all the bits, and either rivet or weld them together confident they will fit. Not so aluminium; the crucial value-add is, in fact, a kind of 'fudge'—making the connections by hand and, it sounds corny to say it, with skill, dedication and love. But talk to the welders in Hobart about their work and you discover that they croon over the ships they build in much the same cooing, gurgling way that a new mother talks about her baby. The workers were even encouraged to make their own toolboxes from aluminium and the stalls in the bathrooms were made from offcuts. Aluminium, along with lightness, became an Incat state of mind. On the surface, this looks like a backwards technical step—after all, the future must lie with the assembly robots? Not with aluminium—the material absolutely reinstates craft skill as the key determinant and, in the process, elevates the skilful craftsperson over every other contributor.

Robert Clifford, therefore, became a kind of ambassador for aluminium in the ship-building world, devoted to the cause that no substantial aluminium ship anywhere in the world should be permitted to go to the bottom of the ocean. Ship-building, like any other trade, is conservative. Having discovered the virtues of steel in the nineteenth century, conventional ship-builders were very resistant to the idea that another alloy might offer multiple advantages to the ship-builder. The real problem for the traditional ship-builder was not that aluminium might burn in a fire (one of the scare stories put out in the past) or suffer from catastrophic metal fatigue, but that making a good ship out of the material demanded the very specialised design-and-build skills of a bunch of eccentrics in Tasmania.

Two consequences flowed from the emergence of Incat—and Robert Clifford—as champions for aluminium. One was that the deals to build the ships overseas were risky because they exposed the aluminium ship in general to reputational risk. If a licensee made a faulty ship which failed—that is, sank—the whole enterprise would be threatened. So the licensing deals had to end. The second consequence was that Incat somehow had to elevate aluminium construction to the higher reaches of technical education. That, in turn, meant a partnership with another arm of government.

During 1988–1991, Incat were constructing three new manu-facturing sheds and, alongside, establishing an entirely new way of training workers and apprentices for the special demands of manufacturing in aluminium. With the sudden growth in produc-tion, Incat had a need for a flexible teaching facility on site so, in the space of just a few months, the Hobart Technical College (part of the TAFE system) was persuaded to second teaching staff to Incat to create a new aluminium welder training school at Prince of Wales

Bay. This meant establishing a certification program—the first of its kind in the world—and persuading the Welding Technology Institute of Australia to establish the examination standards. Very soon they had a first tranche of 50 established apprentices and another 45 trainees, plus a stream of 'Jobtrain' unemployed new entrants passing through the various programs—including high quality training for supervisors.

The new Tasmanian College of Aluminium Training was a good example of Robert Clifford's skill in redesigning the 'upstream' system to serve Incat's needs. The new system quickly became a national and international exemplar. It represented a clever partnership between the interests of the TAFE system (in providing the most relevant and effective training) and Incat (in making sure they produced products of the very highest quality). In no time, every state training body in Australia was making the trip to Hobart to see how it was done. Soon they were helping the Canadians and the Koreans to replicate the system across the seas. Soon the new title 'College of Aluminium Training' mysteriously appeared on the wall outside the main workshop—Robert Clifford's not-so-subtle way of promoting the virtue of the CAT idea.

As a result of the increased overseas interest, Terry Hall (the TAFE teacher who had masterminded the program) realised that other commercial interests—including Incat's fiercest ship-building rivals in Australia—were bound to take advantage of their investment in training by cherry-picking some of the graduates. He raised the issue of competitive advantage, especially of foreign interests, and intellectual property with Robert Clifford. The response was: 'As long as an aluminium ship does not sink anywhere in the world, I will back you as far as you would like to take it.' He was as good as his word.

Eventually, recognising the huge benefits the new facility was bringing to Tasmania, the government agreed to fund the construction of an A$8 million training facility, designed to be the best metal and aluminium fabrication training operation in the world.

By 1997, a new 3500 square metre training centre had 17 teaching staff and 50 welding bays to train 400 apprentices and trainees from all over the world. In addition, the system provided scholarships for other staff to attend the Faculty of Engineering at the University of Tasmania; some of them went on to get doctorates in engineering. Making big complicated cats out of aluminium is both an art and a craft, and Robert Clifford always understood the importance of training in craft skills. He had been, after all, 'apprentice of the year' back in 1960.

22

Big business

Contracting with James Sherwood represented something of a baptism of fire for a smallish Hobart ship-builder. For the first time, a major corporation was beginning to take a serious interest in Robert Clifford's valuable ideas and expertise. In their previous dealings, Sherwood had seemed much like the small businessmen with whom Incat had worked previously. Even the addenda to the formal contract to build a 51-metre vehicle-carrying fast cat for the English Channel crossing (to connect with Sherwood's Orient Express) were handwritten in Sherwood's spidery hand. But the innocent-looking document contained a few clues as to what was to come.

Sherwood was demanding a A$2 million guarantee from the Tasmanian Government to protect his investment in the new infrastructure, which would eventually incorporate the new college on the site to service the specialised workers needed. He also wanted a stake in the Incat company. More worrying still was Sea Containers' interest in the intellectual property. This may be a function of contracting with Americans, because it cropped up again when Incat started to work with the US military in 1999.

The Americans, it seems, feel entitled to buy not just your product but your knowhow as well—perhaps even your company.

Robert Clifford had long since decided that he wasn't interested in the protection of patents—nor in the expensive and drawn-out depredations of lawyers. His motto has always been 'They're welcome to copy what I was doing five years ago!' Speed, both in the water and in pace of change, has always been the Incat driver. It's no surprise therefore that Craig Clifford trained as a lawyer. The firm was always going to need some in-house savvy in relation to intellectual property. The standoff with Sherwood over intellectual property actually led to the cancellation of the first wave-piercer contract; the Sea Containers board wouldn't budge on the commercial protection issues.

By 1988, Sherwood had learned that Robert Clifford could not be bullied into anything. He also knew he still wanted a fast, vehicle-carrying wave-piercer for the development of his ferry businesses, so there was going to have to be a compromise. It was a delicately balanced business relationship. But by that time Sherwood and Incat had carried out exhaustive tank tests in a specialised facility in Vienna. Clifford, as usual relying on the ocean as his test-bed, thought it was a waste of time, but Sherwood wisely insisted. The tests did indeed prove that their wave-piercer design still had a vulnerability to nose-diving in following seas (remember the *Tassie Devil 2001*'s bar landing on Robert's head). As a result, the first big wave-piercer had considerable additional buoyancy built into its bow.

That aborted contract had been signed in May 1987. Sherwood was back for another try the next year. Robert, meanwhile, was eying up the Irish Sea crossing, with the idea that the Bass Strait crossing to Tasmania could serve as its test-bed—provided the Tasmanian Government bought into the idea. He could see that, with the Bass Strait and Irish Sea conquered, the world was full of sea crossings of a similar kind—all currently served by slow-moving and expensive steel monohulls. He also knew that the world was full of fiercely competitive ferry companies with an urgent need to upgrade their operations. Gradually, Robert Clifford was getting to know them all. Some, intrigued by Incat's ideas and designs, beat a path to his door. Others had to be approached. He was the right man to do so—a genius ship-builder who happened to know all about ferry operations.

By now both Sherwood and Clifford were committed to building a big fast vehicle-carrying catamaran. The deal was finally struck in September 1988—and the new state-of-the-art yard at Prince of Wales Bay (modelled on the Boeing production line) was just about ready for the job—at any rate to make a start—at which point only 60 per cent of the design drawings were completed. Sherwood, with the government's support, actually helped to build the factory around the half-completed boat. This really was a 'just in time' effort. In the meantime, further tank testing and calculation on sea-keeping demonstrated that they had underestimated the ship's mass. The contract with Sherwood was based on performance criteria, not on technical detail—in other words on *outcome* (speed + carrying capacity at sea) not on *output* (a ship). That meant redoubling the effort, in mid-design, to reduce weight wherever possible because for every 50 tonnes of weight they sacrificed 1.25 knots of speed at constant power. That in turn meant replacing steel with aluminium wherever it seemed safe to do so.

But it also meant they were going to have to (still in mid-design) build a bigger boat for vehicle-carrying commercial operations. The contract was amended on the hoof to a 66-metre vessel, later amended to 72 metres and finally 74.9 metres—just double the length of their most recently built commercial ship. All this meant boosting the power of the four Ruston engines to an unprecedented 14.6 megawatts of power, including an extended (and again unprecedented) use of aluminium in the engine parts. The final payload of the craft was 450 people and 84 cars—a huge increase over any previous not-so-fast ferry. In the end, *Christopher Columbus* actually provided more deadweight (cargo carrying capacity) and faster speeds than the contract specified. So they got their sums right—on the hoof.

Once again, Incat had got it more-or-less right first time, just as they had with the first all-aluminium boat (*Fitzroy*) nine years before. *Christopher Columbus* (hull 025) was launched on 28 January 1990. She wasn't perfect; indeed the sea trials were eventful. Not for the last time in a sea trial, Robert Clifford succeeded in putting the beautiful new craft up on rocks in the Derwent River. The problem was an electrical overload which triggered a steering and reversing failure, just at the moment the boost engine started. Further incorrect wiring caused the manoeuvring engine to fire on its own accord and only the emergency stops slowed the ship enough for a soft landing on the rocks. The 230 people on board, including the media (this was Good Friday) didn't feel a thing and wondered why they had stopped so close to the shoreline trees. A tug (embarrassingly) had to pull them off but they took some satisfaction in the minimal damage the two main floats had sustained. Not for the last time, they had inadvertently demonstrated the structural sturdiness of aluminium.

There were also serious problems with vibration in the water-jets—this being the first ever Incat craft equipped with them. On the delivery voyage, a sudden violent vibration announced that one of the water-jet blades had broken. It turned out the other three were similarly at risk due to a casting fault in manufacture. And the engines and ride control gave intermittent trouble. The Incat team worked continuously to put everything right so that the next ship, held back for modifications, was much more reliable on its launch in April 1990. Even then *Hoverspeed France* (hull 026) was held back until the following year so as to learn from the operating experience of hull 025. She finally entered service for the UK summer season of 1991.

Underlying these particular technical difficulties were the challenges presented by the design itself. By doubling the length of a wave-piercer (to get the required capacity), they had increased the tendency of the hulls to twist and turn as they encountered waves, because each bow was absorbing pressure from different directions at different times, thus distorting the whole vessel. Nick Wells, Incat's Project Manager, reflected on the implications of the sudden jump from 37 to 74 metres:

> The ocean surface is a dynamic and turbulent environment. We could run tank tests and create computer simulations of the ship's 'hot spots' (areas of significant stress and potential fatigue) but there was a great deal of uncertainty. No one had built a three-hulled aluminium catamaran before. Even after construction began, we couldn't be sure the design was right. (correspondence, 2009)

In June 1991, *Hoverspeed France* (hull 026) finally set off to Southampton via Fremantle, Mauritius, Djibouti and Messina, after a couple of trial runs to Melbourne and Sydney. She was bound for Sea Containers' Portsmouth to Cherbourg route. In October 1990, Incat had launched *SeaCat Tasmania*, designed for the Bass Strait run where the service started at the end of the year. She progressed eventually to the River Plate in Argentina as *Atlantic II*. In just over a year, they had three of the big fast cats in successful operation. Incat had graduated to big business.

23

Doubling up

The whole history of Robert Clifford's endeavour has been characterised by the building of bigger and bigger ships. The trick has been to gain the carrying-capacity advantages of size while preserving the distinctive Incat virtues of lightness, wave-piercing and speed. It looks like a classic example of continuous and incremental improvement (*kaizen*)—but that extraordinary overnight leap in waterline length from 37 metres to 74 metres is the romantic bit. The romance of physics means that a doubling in length delivers an *eight*-times increase in volume—and that means a whole new kind of beast. Gregory Bateson, in his *Mind and Nature* (1979), reminds us how extraordinary this was—not that they built a much bigger ship, but that it worked at all:

> They say the Nobel people are still embarrassed when anybody mentions polyploid horses . . . Dr P.U. Posif . . . got his prize . . . for jiggling with the DNA of the common carthorse (*Equus caballus*) . . . [by] creating . . . a horse precisely twice the size of an ordinary Clydesdale. It was twice as long, twice as high and twice as thick. It was a polyploid, with four times the usual number of chromosomes.

P.U. Posif always claimed that there was a time, when this wonderful animal was still a colt, when it was able to stand on its four legs. A wonderful sight it must have been! But anyhow, by the time the horse was shown to the public . . . [it] was not doing any standing. In a word, it was too heavy. It weighed, of course, eight times as much as a normal Clydesdale.

For a public showing and for the media, Dr Posif always insisted on turning off the hoses that were continually necessary to keep the beast at normal mammalian temperature. But we were always afraid that the innermost parts would begin to cook. After all, the poor beast's skin and dermal fat were twice as thick as normal, and its surface area was only four times that of a normal horse, so it didn't cool properly.

Every morning, the horse had to be raised to its feet with the aid of a small crane and hung in a sort of box on wheels, in which it was suspended on springs, adjusted to take half its weight off its legs.

Dr Posif used to claim that the animal was outstandingly intelligent. It had, of course, eight times as much brain (by weight) as any other horse, but I could never see that it was concerned with any questions more complex than those that interest other horses. It had very little free time, what with one thing and another—always panting, partly to keep cool and partly to oxygenate its eight-times body. Its windpipe, after all, had only four times the normal area of cross section.

And then there was eating. Somehow it had to eat, every day, eight times the amount that would satisfy a normal horse and had to push all that food down an oesophagus only four times the calibre of the normal. The blood vessels, too, were reduced in relative size, and this made circulation more difficult and put extra strain on the heart.

A sad beast.

You could not have arrived at a workable, twice-size vessel on mathematical extrapolation and tank testing alone. As soon as he had absorbed the lessons of the Boeing production process, Clifford had grasped that they were moving beyond ship-building to a new place. But it was a place where only sailors and other intuitive, trial-and-error types could go. There were no maps of the new terrain. *Hoverspeed Great Britain* didn't work perfectly at first—but she worked well enough to establish a new market, to race over the Atlantic faster than any passenger-carrying vessel before and to demonstrate that calculation and tank testing are not enough.

24

The Santa Fe Railroad question

A traditional case study in the business school world is that of the Santa Fe Railroad. The company went broke because it believed it was in the railroad business; it always had been in the past, but things had moved on. Its managers were confusing *outputs* (railroad journeys) with *outcomes* (transportation solutions and customer experience). What the market needed was the efficacious movement of goods and people around the United States and it didn't much care how it was done. The railroad might be one solution to the problem but by no means the only or best one. What matters is what the potential customer needs. Robert Clifford had learned that principle from supplying crayfish to restaurateurs, user-friendliness to ferry operators, agreeable journeys-to-work to commuters and now by supplying the perfect way to enhance a mad, romantic journey on the Venice–Simplon Orient Express. Whatever it takes.

That extraordinary year of 1989, when the world of ferry transport was transformed forever, must be attributed to three rather remarkable men working well together for a while—James Sherwood as ferry operator, Robert Clifford as boat-builder and

Philip Hercus—on board the enterprise since 1978—as principal designer. This is what they call synergy in the business schools; it could not have happened without pooling and intermingling the special skills of all three men. Hercus, however, was in the process of falling out comprehensively with Sherwood, because he had had grave doubts not only about the sudden leap to much bigger craft but also about the manageability of a business relationship with Sea Containers.

Clifford and Sherwood, by comparison, seemed to many people like a pair of big ego-driven bull elephants trumpeting around the jungle, although in reality their relationship was much more like that between the Clifford father and son (Fred and Robert)—tempestuous on the surface but still, for a while, creative. Robert Clifford shared Hercus' concerns about contracting with Sea Containers and with Sherwood; he was simply prepared to take the risk in order to secure the bigger prize of the higher-order momentum of fast ferry development. This shows how Clifford is an inventor first and a businessman second. Finding out what works, or what can be made to happen, always trumps mundane business calculation. The Incat–Sea Containers business relationship did eventually end in tears, but the risk turned out to be worth it. For Clifford, getting into bed with Sherwood was a 'judgement call'—evidently risky but probably worth it long term.

Perhaps the collaboration with Sherwood had another downside as it persuaded Robert Clifford that business relations with big firms can be conducted successfully on the basis of vigorous bargaining with an individual entrepreneur, sealed with a handshake and a minimal contract. Sherwood was a big business man who still behaved like the go-getting entrepreneurs with whom Clifford had always dealt. Clifford still had to learn about the tortuous and often political ways that big firms go about contracting with their suppliers. That sort of contracting demanded subtlety and patience—not attributes most people attributed to Clifford.

By the beginning of 1988, Philip Hercus had had enough. His view of the Santa Fe Railroad question—or in modern parlance the 'business model'—differed fundamentally from Clifford's. He was a distinguished naval architect so he took the view that the real 'unique selling proposition' lay in the designs. Clifford, inspired by the links with Boeing, was absolutely certain the true value-add lay in the specialised manufacturing skills they were developing. Anybody, he reasoned, could design a ship, and skilled designers were notoriously mobile, but nobody else in the world knew how to make these very special ships. Accordingly, after a very fruitful 10-year partnership, Clifford and Hercus split the business amicably; the licences went to Sydney with Hercus as Incat Designs and the manufacturing stayed in Hobart as Incat Tasmania. But the achievement of the big cat took all three of them—Hercus, Clifford and Sherwood.

As it turned out, Robert Clifford's idea was right if your main criterion is business success. Three years later, Robert recreated the design facility in Hobart and repatriated some of the best draughtsmen. And many years later, the Sea Containers group of companies ended up seeking Chapter 11 (bankruptcy) protection, in 2006. Hercus Designs continues as a niche or boutique player in nautical design, but only Incat conquered the world. Sherwood was happiest wheeling and dealing (until he took on one deal too many), Hercus was meant by fate to design ships and Robert Clifford, as we have seen, was raised up to invent, make and do. The money Incat has made for its principal shareholders is impressive but that was never the main point; it remains a by-product of the quest to perfect the ships. This makes Clifford a very unusual businessman.

25

Incat culture

Tasmania is a small island and Hobart (for a capital city) is a small town of around 200 000 people. The main Incat yard is close to the centre of town and the presence or absence of the huge completed ships sitting in Prince of Wales Bay is inescapable to any passer-by. So everybody in Hobart always knows the state of the global fast ferry market. By the end of the 1980s, Robert Clifford was in the process of becoming a local celebrity. His habit of running big ships on rocks in the Derwent River (there was more to come) simply cemented a swashbuckling reputation first established when the bridge went down. And, increasingly, the Tasmanian economy depended on Incat's expanding workforce and export earnings. In the circumstances, it would have been difficult to evade any sort of celebrity but Robert understood from the start that the institution Incat was inseparable from Robert Clifford the man—he might as well play the part properly.

By the end of the 1980s, Incat was established as a major regional player in specialised ship-building and was beginning to assume the nucleus role within the Tasmanian Light Shipbuilding Cluster. As such, it was to become a kind of mother ship to a range of 'upstream' suppliers in marine fire equipment, foundry machining, life-raft systems, marine industrial hydraulics and other specialised technologies and trades—all supported by the educational infrastructure of the Australian Maritime College and the co-located TAFE College of Aluminium Training. It was as if Incat was spawning a small town on the sprawling Prince of Wales Bay site.

Professor Michael Porter of Harvard was one of the pioneers of the study of industrial clusters in his famous book *The Competitive Advantage of Nations* (1990). His argument was that governments are generally bad at 'picking winners' for direct financial support; however, they always have the potential to improve their capacity to determine the combination of factors—material, financial and social—which sometimes leads to great commercial success within particular industries. Having done the determination, governments can then act as catalyst and challenger of the actual or potential cluster members.

One of Porter's examples, highly relevant to Incat and Tasmania in the 1980s, was the hugely successful North Italian ceramic tile industry—characterised by fierce competition between hundreds of smallish firms and a form of industry-wide technical and educational collaboration promoted by regional and national government. Porter thus put paid to the old and crude distinction between competition and collaboration—as if human beings have to make a stark choice between fighting other people or befriending them. The Italian ceramic tile industry was a good example of both—a complementary interaction between a tooth-and-claw private sector and public support for social and intellectual infrastructure in the form of research institutes, training colleges and the like: a 'mixed economy', in other words.

The trick for government is to intervene in the private sector in the right way and at the right time—always to preserve the resilience of the local system. Italian central and regional governments got it right in the tile industry. A contemporary example of central government muddling the centre/local issue is provided by the Federal Government's sale of Bankstown Airport to big business. The airport has evolved naturally over many years to become an important part of Australia's aviation infrastructure—supporting an inter-related 'cluster' of service providers in light aircraft delivery, servicing and pilot training—an important contributor to the economy and the nation's technical bona fides internationally. When banks become owners of infrastructure they tend to argue they have a duty to their shareholders to maximise short-term financial gains and that means (if the bit of infrastructure is a regional airport) treating an airport as if it were merely a property development. And that, in turn, is likely to kill off the interlinked small firms at the airport which keep the nation's aviation infrastructure intact.

Michael Porter points out that the Italians succeeded in balancing the interests of big and small business (the 'level playing field') and looking after the longer term strategic interest. Australian governments, juggling the strategic interest between Commonwealth and State, have a patchy record, as Bankstown demonstrates. In the case of Incat, although Robert Clifford sometimes grumbles, there has been timely financial support from government in the interest of securing a strategically important regional industrial hub. Incat is a private company which has benefited from judicious public support over the years; notably in the financial backing of the wave-piercer prototypes. The integration of strategic support fell down spectacularly in 2002, but that story is still to come.

Hobart, it turned out, had something like the right combination of Porter's 'factors'. Firstly, it had a deeply embedded ship-building culture and a multiplicity of boatyards and associated craftspersons. The first boat was built in Hobart within a few days of the first European settlement in 1803. Even now, the old boat-building traditions are celebrated in a biennial international Wooden Boat Festival. This proud history is celebrated in the names of the enormous ship-building sheds on Incat's Hobart site, each one named after one of the state's early boat-builders—Gunn's, Inches,

McGregor, Coverdale's, Degrave's and, the biggest of all, Wilson's. There was another place in Australia with a similar profile—the Henderson area near Perth—and that was home to the firm that would become Incat's fiercest downunder competitor: Austal Ships Ltd. Like Incat, Austal Ships had arisen from an old boat-building tradition based on yachting and fishing—and especially the building of fast boats to garner rock lobsters. (Somebody should point out to Professor Porter the crucial importance of crustaceans in the structural formation of both of the world-beating fast-ship builders that emerged in late twentieth century Australia.)

Secondly, in Robert Clifford and Incat, Hobart had a firm with a keen understanding of Porter's 'demand conditions'—in this case the needs of an important and developing niche in international shipping. Robert Clifford was getting to know the proprietors of all the main operators of ferries in all the world's waterways suitable for fast ferry services. And, as an ex-ferryman, he was getting to understand their business needs now and in the future. In the west, Austal Ships likewise could build on its experience in aluminium construction, driven by Alan Bond's successive attempts on the America's Cup yacht races.

Thirdly, Hobart had a cluster of firms in the process of rapidly responding to Incat's demand for upstream products and services. And, perhaps most important of all, it had an army of yachtsmen well used to fierce, sometimes brutal, competition, but supported by the rules of yacht racing and the conviviality of the Derwent Sailing Squadron and the city's other yachting clubs. Hobart is a yachting city and is the destination of one of the world's great ocean yacht races. The fiftieth Sydney–Hobart race was won by Robert Clifford in 1994, but that's another story.

A good part of Incat's success must be put down to this intense comradeship and loyalty among sailors within its professional, managerial and technical ranks. It's not quite true to say that the senior ranks of Incat are closed to non-sailors, but it is true to say that sometimes too much loyalty to old colleagues has got in the way of painful, timely decisions. This sense of mutual obligation is a key part of the 'social capital' that Porter draws attention to. To understand its power, it is probably necessary to visit Hobart and, in particular, the 'Shipwright's Arms'—Incat's informal 'office'. It's just the pub up the road from Clifford's Hobart residence but it's the place where the Hales Trophy was displayed and where the man can still be found surrounded by Incat stalwarts after a day at the other (registered) office. As Porter recognised, culture is crucial in success; Incat has a formal registered office and headquarters, but its true culture demands a 'real' HQ in a sailors' pub.

In a 2008 interview with Jennifer Alexander of the Australian Institute of Management, Robert Clifford responded to a question about Australianness in Incat culture:

I think being a Tasmanian has an effect because we are an island culture. Everything we need comes in and out by water; most of our staff own a boat. They're maritime people; that maritime culture is important. I think if we lived in Parramatta or Sydney it wouldn't be the same . . . Our customers also come from similar backgrounds . . . We sell to island communities around the world!

It is an intensely loyal culture but also a no-nonsense one. Stuart Florence, formerly Incat's personnel manager, has kept a copy of a characteristically trenchant memorandum from Robert Clifford to all the company's employees in 1989, just at the perilous moment the firm was about to lift off to the next level of international operations. It captures nicely the quality of the Incat culture—a sort of indication of its DNA, extracted from the bloodstream of its founder:

Dear Employee,

On Friday last I reported to all shareholders the results of the financial year ended June 1989. I now wish to bring you up to date. We made a reasonable profit for the year, having finished one boat for New Zealand and contracted to build two for the UK and one for Tasmanian Ferry Services.

Unfortunately cash is extremely tight as we have all our money tied up in the vessels under construction.

I know of lots of urgently needed improvements like more toilets, better lunch places etc. We also need more equipment, welders, cranes, but the money is just not there to buy them and we have to seriously consider the priority of each item.

You will have noticed the steady stream of suited gentlemen I have been showing through the works, trying to impress them to advance us more money. Until I am successful we must try hard to reduce stock and maximise the use of offcuts etc. and make do with the equipment we have got.

When the first vessel passes her sea trials and we are fully paid, finances will improve a bit and we will be able to attend to the workshop and conditions, until then don't be surprised to see me and other managers helping out on the tools.

You have probably heard that the main engines will be late, this does not help, as the later we finish the first vessel the later we get paid. Therefore we are re-scheduling the installation of all equipment so that we can minimise the delay. Incidentally, if the first boat does not pass her trials there is no point in worrying about the second and third as we will be out of business and you will be out of work.

The boat will be successful, I have no doubt about that, but we are not on a picnic and I expect all hands to carry their share of the load. Eighty percent are doing just that and I am very pleased with the majority. There are, however, 10% just going along for the ride and there are 10% just plain bludging. They will not be with us for long.

Anyone who tells you that you are due for increases like the airline pilots is dreaming. There is only one way we can pay more money and that is to increase production, that is if we build more, we can sell more and we can pay more. It's pretty simple really.

When this happens we will be in good shape and the profits will be shared. Until then, dream on, but not in company time.

When we are successful I have no intention of being the richest man in the cemetery. Last year I sold some of my company shares to 40 others who have now received their first dividend. I want this company to be ours not mine so at the meeting last Friday it was decided to offer another 100 $1 shares to all employees. The offer will close at the end of September so you have four weeks to find the money if you wish to take up the shares offer.

In approximately six months time it is intended to repeat the offer. If you are interested in a greater number of shares you should state your case and it will be considered.

I would like to think that you will take this memo home to discuss the contents with your wife [*sic*] and family as the decisions you make over the next few weeks could have long term consequences.

I take the future of our company very seriously and am prepared to take the hard decisions if they are in the best interests of us all.

Don't hesitate to talk to me or other management if you have any doubts or queries. I need to know if you have a problem.

Regards,

Robert Clifford

Chief Shareholder and Managing Director

PART FOUR

Playing with the big boys

Anatomy of a maturing, global business

26

You couldn't make it up

The successful construction and sale of *Christopher Columbus* (later *Hoverspeed Great Britain*) launched Incat on 10 years of unbroken success in a market that the company had essentially created. In a sense, the 1990s were thus a kind of scaled-up rerun of the seven-year period after the success of *Fitzroy*, the first all-aluminium boat in 1980. That run of success was preceded by a slump in Incat fortunes (waiting nervously for the market to catch up with Incat's ideas) and followed by another slump in the late 1980s when the market for fast cats in Queensland became saturated. By then Clifford could see that further growth had to be on the international stage, hence the rather grand title 'International Catamarans'. The reader will see a recurrent pattern here—Incat racing ahead with design and technological leadership, and sometimes racing a bit too fast and far for the customers. (It happened again, famously, in 2002.)

So the history of Incat up until 1990 had been something of a roller-coaster ride—and in many ways an unlikely tale. Robert Clifford's invention of the big, wave-piercing, aluminium fast ferry represents a good moment to stop and reflect on the story thus far. The key word is 'story': this is a kind of biography but in truth it is a narrative with peaks and troughs, interrupted by extraordinary events. As they say in journalism: 'You couldn't make it up!' If this was fiction, the collapse of the Derwent River bridge would be a plot-twist too far. The great Robert McKee, author of the dramatists' and screen-writers' bible, *Story: Substance, Structure, Style and the Principles of Screenwriting*, suggests that it is pointless to argue for the supremacy of either character or plot in telling a compelling story (1990). Aristotle thought that story was the primary element, character secondary, but that was at a time when the gods seemed to call most of the shots. The modern view is that 'character-driven' drama is most gripping.

McKee might look on the winning of the Blue Riband in 1990 as merely a romantic plot twist. This wasn't just any old record to be broken but one of the iconic records—dating from the sail-powered 'clipper' runs in the mid-nineteenth century. The quickest ship in those days got to fly a blue pennant from its mainsail then, in 1935, Sir Harold Hales (the owner of Hales Brothers Shipping) instigated the magnificently kitsch 1.2 metres high trophy of gilded silver. The list of holders of the trophy reads like a history of the great ships—*Lusitania, Normandie, Queen Mary* and finally, in 1952, the USS *United States* at about 35 knots.

Then a fast ferry built by a Tasmanian butcher's son joined the hallowed ranks of the Blue Riband holders. You couldn't make it up—especially when you saw the gilded monstrosity (with a couple of security guards discreetly in tow) perched on the bar of the Shipwright's Arms. But the Hales Trophy was more than a plot twist; it was Robert Clifford's idea that Incat and Sea Containers might boost their profiles by going for the record. James Sherwood didn't take much persuading, but it was Margaret Thatcher who more or less insisted that the Bermuda-registered craft should have Great Britain incorporated in its name so it could be presented as a British triumph. The great Anglophile Sherwood was happy to oblige.

There is no doubt that Robert Clifford is a 'character'—and had been so since infancy. Anybody born with such single-minded determination and extraordinary talents will make some kind of mark on the world, especially if he has a cavalier approach to risk. That bravery or foolhardiness ensures that he will repeatedly thrust himself into character-forming and character-testing situations. As McKee notes: 'True character is revealed in the choices a human being makes under pressure—the greater the pressure, the deeper the revelation, the truer the choice to the character's essential nature.' By this point in the story, just as the hero is about to launch himself on the world (fast ferry) stage, the reader should have been fed enough hints about his underlying character to know that it might lead to disaster—and to want to read on.

Read again the extraordinary 1989 letter to all Incat staff. Robert Clifford, we must recall, was no good at school subjects, including, as a dyslexic, studies in the English language. Yet this letter has the pungency of poetry, an intimation of drama—and it reveals character. Before they started brawling (creatively), one of the favourite pastimes of father and young son (Fred and Robert) was reading poetry together. In the letter to staff, the reference to 'suited gentlemen' establishes him as a man of the people; the pointed reference to sea trials injects a dramatic reminder about the real world out there (if the ship fails, *everybody* is out of a job); the statement 'I have no doubt the boat will succeed' then reassures; the remarks about 'bludgers' is a frightener and introduces the dramatic threat of the enemy within; the reference to the 'richest man in the cemetery' is a personal credo about fairness and sharing; and the final statement of his preparedness to shoulder the 'hard decisions' asserts leadership in the bluntest of terms.

The fact that the letter is reproduced in an early company history tells us that this is a piece of self-expression or self-promotion with which the central hero (of the unfolding story) is comfortable. Robert

Clifford has always been comfortable with the idea that he is the central character in an unfolding drama and that his actions—from ritually stalking the quayside to cast off the ropes on every new ship's delivery voyage to writing personally to all the staff—speak louder than any PR department's press releases. The problem for a biographer rests in Robert McKee's dictum that 'Movies are about their last twenty minutes.' The end of a good story resolves the relationship between structure and character, making it clear that they are much the same thing—character determines story and story determines character. But the Incat story isn't over yet. At least the reader can be assured that the central character is destined to live an exciting life.

27

Incat grows up

Back in 1989—the year Incat graduated to the big time—there were pitfalls aplenty facing the company. This is the point when many enterprises fail, when the complexity of operations increases exponentially. Incat, after all, had been a smallish Hobart boat-builder used to dealing with not-too-sophisticated domestic customers, suddenly confronted with new kinds of dealings with very big international firms—but now building ships twice as long as the biggest of the 1988 output. Clifford's preferred way of doing business had always been a boisterous sort of negotiation with a man like himself, followed by a handshake. There would be a formal contract, but the essence lay in mutual trust between equals. Big business doesn't think or act much like that. Yet over the next 10 years, Incat succeeded in producing and selling a constantly evolving series of beautiful ships, all of which exceeded the expectations of their new big business owners. Indeed, the big, fast wave-piercer succeeded in transforming the international customers' businesses in exactly the same way that *Fitzroy* and her successors transformed the homely Barrier Reef tourist trade.

How could this have come about? At the heart was a genius conceptualiser and designer. Over the years, the engineers at Incat have got used to the boss alighting from an aircraft with new design ideas, which are nearly always productive. Robert Clifford has always taken pride in the fact that his ideas on the back of an envelope usually turn out to be soundly based once the designers feed them into the computers. So something is going on in that brain which parallels the processing power of big computers. It was no different at Hutchins School, where the teachers thought he was a dunce and couldn't believe he had built a good boat single-handedly in his bedroom. Even then he used to intuit the answers in maths lessons without going through all the tortuous steps of mathematical computation. It is a form of inductive, rather than deductive, reasoning.

So it is no surprise that Incat was a very early adopter of the most advanced CAD/CAM methods. Computer-aided design and manufacture actually mimic the activity of a model-builder like Robert Clifford. What the computer programs provide is analogous to the physical manipulation of three-dimensional real-world objects. The designer sitting at his screen can turn the representation of the object over, spin it around, even view it from the inside. In his childhood and youth, Robert Clifford never embarked on a project without lovingly constructing a model first. When Incat got into big ships he understood intuitively that CAD/CAM was more than just a design tool, it was an extension of his imaginative world—a way of scaling up while hanging on to the old craft skills and native intuition. Computer modelling may provide part of the answer to Dick Smith's question: How did he do it? It is hard to see how, in just a few years, you get from smallish boats to very sophisticated big ships (where the main component parts are as big as the boats) without CAD/CAM.

This is exciting, leading-edge stuff but there is a mundane side to it; if every ship you build is different because you are constantly introducing innovations and improvements, then you will need a meticulous record of every member, every joint, every bracket; in practice, even every weld has to be documented in the drawings, models and in the supporting documentation relating to every ship.

The infant inventor, about to carry out an early experiment – smashing the first birthday cake.

The skipper, aged 16, surveys the cost of sailing too close to the wind – a broken lightweight mast – too lightweight.

APPRENTICE OF YEAR

Apprentice of the year in 1961 (aged 18 years). (Courtesy of *The Mercury*, Hobart)

ROBERT F. CLIFFORD, an 18-year-old apprentice compositor, was yesterday named "Apprentice of the Year" for 1961.

The announcement was made by the president of the Printing and Allied Trades Employers' Association (Mr. J. W. Anderson).

Robert, of East Risdon Rd., Bellerive, is employed by Mr. J. M. Newman, of Specialty Press, and was selected from 28 entrants.

The prize is a five-day trip to Melbourne, and a book suited to his trade. He was also presented with a cheque for £5 by the Government Printer (Mr. L. G. Shea) on behalf of the State Government.

In making the announcement, Mr. Anderson remarked on the high grade of efficiency attained by the six finalists, this being borne out by their reports from Technical College and employers.

The competitors were judged on these reports, and other headings, a panel of four judges making the final decision.

Winning the award came as a surprise to Robert. He said he had not expected to win, and none of the finalists had any idea of the result until the presentation yesterday.

Mr. Anderson thanked the Director of Education (Mr. Tribolet) for attending the function.

● In the picture Mr. Anderson (left) is seen handing a letter of congratulation to Robert Clifford. At centre is the Director of Education (Mr. D. H. Tribolet).

The boat designer, aged 27 years, with a model of the first trans-Derwent River ferry, the *Matthew Brady*. This marked a decisive break from fishing into constructing and operating ferries.

Tasman Bridge, 5 January 1975. A photograph taken shortly after the freighter *Lake Illawarra* had ploughed through pylons 18 and 19, bringing down 128 metres of the four-lane concrete highway. (Photograph: Don Stephens)

Fitzroy, the first all-aluminium boat, launched on 19 June 1981.

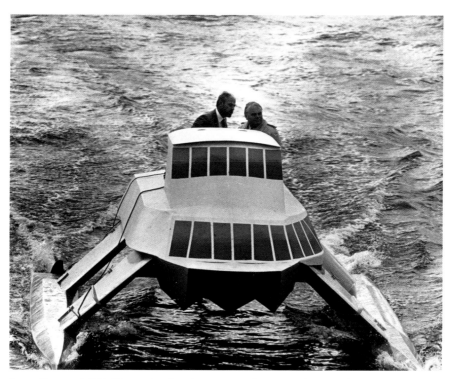

James Sherwood (Chief Executive, Sea Containers Ltd) visits Hobart to ride on *Little Devil* – the wave-piercer prototype in 1983.

The tasteful Hales Trophy, awarded for the fastest crossing of the Atlantic (3 days, 7 hours and 52 minutes) on 23 June 1990, adorns the bar of the Shipwright's Arms (Incat's other 'office') in Battery Point, Hobart.

Robert Clifford's habit of running ships on the Derwent River rocks was always a boon to the local newspaper cartoonists (and the Mr Whippy franchise). (Cartoon by Kev, courtesy Incat)

An Incat-designed craft (R. Clifford the jockey) wins the International Solar Boat Race in 1996 – thus inspiring another inventor to create a new kind of craft.

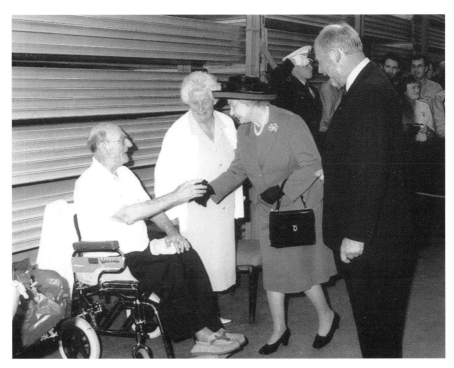

The Queen pays her respects to Eve and Fred Clifford, March 2000.

Ready for action in Kuwait in 2003, HSV-X1 (*Joint Venture* combined services) and TSV-1X (*Spearhead* US Army).

Little and large: *Our Lady Patricia*, Incat's first export ship to the UK (hull 020), leads *Normandie Express* (hull 057) into Portsmouth in 2005. (Photograph: Gary Davies/Maritime Photographic)

Two Samurai warriors (chairman Yamamoto and chairman Clifford) cross-dress at the launching of *Natchan Rera* (the first 112-metre wave-piercer) on 30 June 2007.

The 112-metre *Norman Arrow* at speed on the English Channel (32 big trucks, 200 cars and up to 1200 people at up to 47 knots – nearly 90 kilometres per hour). (Photograph: Bill Burton)

The Clifford Clan assembled in Hobart shortly before the death of Eve Clifford (10 January 2010). Eve is seated at the back, alongside Rohan, Robert Clifford's son by Kerry Sturmey (seated to the right of Robert). Craig is behind his father and Kerry to his left. Seated far left is Robert's brother Tony. Barbara, Robert's ex-wife, can be seen just to the right of Craig.

The new computer systems allowed the Incat system to keep track of all this complexity. This meant the firm was in a position to support its customers by sending them—electronically—solutions to ongoing maintenance or repair problems, because it retained an intimate knowledge of every craft it had ever built.

As the order book lengthened, the firm got bigger—growing very quickly from 350 employees in 1994 to nearly 1000 two years later. So Incat faced the problems of co-ordination and control that all growing firms face. Once again, Clifford didn't need to be told by professors or management consultants that if you organise production around separate lines (so you can build ships in parallel), and you compartmentalise each ship into separate sub-assemblies, then you must put somebody in charge of each subsystem and make him (rarely her) accountable for the outputs of that subsystem. It looks obvious but it is surprising how many organisations neglect these basic rules of operation, especially when they are growing quickly.

Once you approach the thousand people mark, you are obliged to move to a 'stratum-4' organisational system—where the overall boss is going to be three steps removed hierarchically from the welders who are assembling the ships. The test is often whether the boss, however approachable, can remember all the names. Things are simpler in an Australian hard-hat area, as the names are emblazoned on the hats and everybody's name is 'mate' anyway. There is persuasive research which suggests that Australian businesses are world-competitive up to about 1000 people in terms of return on assets, but much less so when the business moves to 'stratum-5' and beyond (Ruthven, *Leadership and Success in Corporate Australia*, IBIS Business Papers, 1994). The Australian 'mateship' culture, it seems, doesn't adapt well to the formalisation required. Australians tend to confuse authority with autocracy and authoritarianism. Never forget, Hobart was originally a particularly brutal convict colony and there are collective folk memories of the worst kinds of 'authority figure'. Clifford got the formal structures

111

right, intuitively, but clung to the human connectedness—nobody could predict for sure where he might pop up—with strong opinions about how things ought to be done. One employee put it clearly: 'Robert draws the organisation chart as a 1000 lines coming off the central spoke.'

28

The Clifford style

As to the Clifford 'management style', Trevor Hardstaff, another long-serving Incat stalwart and one-time shipyard director, offered an insider's view in 1998:

Robert has a similarly informal approach to business negotiations. He rarely enters into written contracts, preferring agreements to be verbal. This allows him to argue like hell during the negotiation stage to get a good price. Having said this, he will honour any bill presented thereafter. Rules, regulations and authorities are not, in my experience, high on Robert's list of favourite things. He has little regard for those rules and regulations he considers to be pointless, misguided or wrong. Obviously this does not include the rules and regulations he creates himself. Over the years he has had some memorable disagreements with local government authorities and public servants. While he might not win the battle, through sheer persistence, Robert always seems to win the war. Robert has a blatant disregard for weekends and public holidays and expects a fair day's work for a fair day's pay. Although he often conveys his disapproval by ranting and raving, I've never known him to sack anyone for not doing their job.

Anybody with the advantage of watching Robert's upbringing at the hands of his father Fred would understand how this kind of management style might evolve. Robert and Fred ranted and raved virtually all the time, but always with the underpinning of family loyalty and love and a strong *materfamilias* in Eve Clifford holding the ring in the background. If you were family, the ranting didn't really count, and especially not if 'the bastard'—your son—was acknowledged to be a 'genius'. As Incat culture evolved, you could expect plenty of ranting from the boss and plenty of high expectations too. But so long as you were family—that is, dedicated to Incat's cause—you could expect almost undying loyalty in return. The events of 2002, still to come, show what happens when this kind of lawlessness as to formal rules and institutions collides with family-like loyalty between people. It is a volatile mixture, but Clifford had long since developed the habit of sailing close to the wind.

So it didn't much matter if you were a member of the Clifford family or of the extended Incat 'family' beyond—your treatment would be pretty much the same. Robert Clifford's 'style' (maybe logic would be a better description than style) is to communicate only when strictly necessary and with the minimum of words for the task in hand. Some people find it a bit abrupt, shorn as it is of any 'small talk'. When Robert Clifford first went to Hutchins School he was under strict instructions from his father to keep his nose clean with all those middle-class kids. Unsurprisingly, he was bullied mercilessly. When the story came out that evening, Fred had to amend the instructions: 'Well, I didn't mean not to defend yourself against those thugs!' The following morning, the sturdy young Clifford repaid the bullies with interest. He turned out to be a champion swimmer at school, but when his mother Eve asked how a particular swimming meet went, the reply was: 'Not too bad.' For the following week, friends and acquaintances bailed her up in the street to offer their congratulations. It turned out Robert had won most of the races and broken a few records to boot. You could call it taciturn.

Something similar happened when young Robert went for his first post-school job. They turned him down because he didn't ask any questions: 'But there wasn't anything else I wanted to know.' Craig Clifford has vivid memories of his twenty-fifth birthday. As usual, he and his father were on opposite sides of the world. The certainty was that he would receive a phone call on the big day—the old man never forgot. The other certainty was that the communication would be affectionately gruff. Robert: 'So, I think it's your birthday. How old are you?' Craig: 'Twenty-five!' Robert: 'Mmmm, that's about when I started losing my hair. Enjoy your day!' Par for the course. In its way, it is an appealing style; at any rate, an honest one. However, it is arguable whether or not it is always the best way to communicate with or to persuade clients who happen to have their own opinions about what kind of ship they need—or whether they ought to be buying a ship at all. And, in 2002, it turned out to be an unhelpful way to communicate with bankers in the course of a financial crisis.

This dislike of any fripperies extends to public events and dress. Robert Clifford knew he had to put on a suit to meet the Queen, but all other occasions are governed by the simple rule that a ship-builder in a shipyard ought to wear working clothes at all times. The dislike of formality extends to all social events such as cocktail parties and formal dinners, and he has been known to attend city meetings with government ministers wearing the better sort of shipyard attire. Of course, there is a method in this eccentricity—it is a very effective way of underlining the negligible 'power distance' between the Incat big boss/company owner and the humble Incat welder. And then there is the trademark wide-brimmed Aussie hat. If the health and safety legislation decrees a hard hat in the shipyard, then the boss will need a specially made *hard* wide-brimmed Akubra—a bit of theatre really.

There is a genuine dislike of poshness and the 'suits' who rule big business, but this is turned to advantage in image-making. Nothing is wasted in Incat. And it fits in with a genuine parsimoniousness in relation to everything from aluminium off-cuts to petty change. Craig Clifford remembers a visit with his father to sign off a A$40 million contract of sale for one of the vessels in the mid 1990s. This entailed a short trip from the Sydney CBD to North Sydney—just the other side of the harbour. Emerging from his office at about 6.00 pm, Craig automatically hailed a cab. This was the signal for Robert to bellow: 'What are you doing? The train station's not far away and it's a hell of a lot cheaper!'

29

'Improving the breed'

The first three 74-metre cats completed in 1990 established the market for the next three years. The subsequent 74-metre craft penetrated the seaways of France (*Hoverspeed France*), Denmark (*Hoverspeed Denmark*), Scotland (*Hoverspeed Scotland*), South America (*Patricia Olivia* and *Juan L*), New Zealand (*Condor 10*), Wales and Ireland (Stena Line's *Sea Lynx*) and the Australian states of Tasmania and Victoria (*SeaCat Tasmania*). In 1993, *SeaCat Tasmania* was taken over by James Sherwood's Sea Containers for the English Channel crossing and subsequently switched, renamed *Atlantic II*, to the River Plate crossing from Buenos Aires to Colonia del Sacramento and Montevideo, thus invading the territory of Incat's long-term customer Buquebus. They got their revenge in the end by buying the company that Sherwood chartered to. But the entry of the fast ferries to the River Plate transformed local transport and made heavy inroads into the air traffic between Argentina and Uruguay. It was actually quicker to go from the centre of town to the ferry terminal and then to arrive in the centre of Montevideo (with your car) than it was to drive to the airport and cope with parking, check-in and all the other hassles of air travel. Quite suddenly, these big fast ships were showing their paces and demonstrating their 'green' credentials—and the world's ferry operators were taking note.

Then, in 1991, tragedy when Robert's father Fred took one too many risks with his beloved animals. When he was 79, one of his racing trotters kicked him in the chest, leaving him severely reduced in activity and ranting levels. It was exactly the kind of accident to be expected of the indefatigable Fred, but it was a reminder that Robert was now approaching 50 years of age and there was the succession to be thought about. Both of his children from the marriage with Barbara—Craig and Kim—were pursuing careers elsewhere. Craig had moved to Sydney in 1990 and was practising as a solicitor for the Sydney firm of Harris & Co., although mostly on Incat legal matters. The founder of that firm John Harris joined the family (the Incat board) in 1995 and took over the ship-building side of the business in 2002 as managing director. Kim was working for BHP in Melbourne on the chartering of ships, having pursued a cookery apprenticeship with a view to cooking professionally. She evidently inherited the Clifford urge to make and do. So the kids had flown the coop but the siren voice of Incat sounded still. Both of them knew, sort of, they would probably be called to duty in due course. It was and is that sort of family.

Robert's younger brother Tony had been caught up in all the early boat-building developments, everybody was, but made his main career in Hydro Tasmania (the state-owned electricity generator) as a controller of power stations throughout Tasmania. When he retired from that, he reverted (perhaps inevitably) to Incat to work for 15 years in a variety of management roles, including head of human resources—no doubt an emollient presence alongside the sometimes abrasive Robert. Robert's sister Anne quit Tasmania completely, but ended up working in a business run in Melbourne by Barbara, Robert's ex-wife (once she finally got away from Tasmania; something she had planned back in 1975 before the bridge went down). Everybody stayed in close touch. Rohan Clifford, Robert's son by Kerry Sturmey, would come into the business in the late 1990s, to work in a variety of technical roles.

And all the while the ships were adapting. *Condor 10,* launched in September 1992, was the first ship to be fitted with a forward 'T-foil' ride control system. Catamarans are subject to special forms of pitch, roll and yaw, which meant that the company had to come up with novel solutions in the interests of passenger comfort. The first cats on the Weymouth to Channel Islands run were subject to a relentless half-on swell rolling in from the Atlantic which meant a queasy combination of pitch, yaw, roll and (appropriately) heave as the waves progressed from one float to the other. Some impolite passengers dubbed the boat the 'vomit comet'. Something had to be done. The answer was the invention of the T-foil. In time, it would be retractable according to sea conditions, not bolted permanently on, and augmented by trim tabs. Soon, T-foils were retro-fitted to the entire fleet.

The origins of the T-foil are typical of the inventiveness and originality of the company during the 1990s. The design for the T-foil (like many Incat innovations) was first drawn on a napkin at the Shipwright's Arms and subsequently developed in partnership with Maritime Dynamics Industries—another family company—of Maryland, United States. Maritime Dynamics had been set up in 1972 by a group of aerospace and marine engineers interested in air cushion and ground-effect craft of special relevance to the US Navy, so they were natural allies for Incat, who were building marine craft in the same way as aeroplanes and whose owner was already experimenting with very fast ground-effect vessels on the Derwent River. Maritime Dynamics is therefore another supplier/ partner profoundly affected by Incat's quest for perfection. During the 1990s when they were getting involved with Robert Clifford, Maritime Dynamics switched from a navy-only clientele towards almost entirely private-sector activity in the high-speed ferry world. They had joined the club.

The development of the T-foil also owed something to the yachting experience of its inventors. Nick Wells, soon to become Incat's head of US military operations, explains the history:

> We had sensors on the front seats of the ship to estimate the number of people that would get seasick. We wanted to improve the numbers, so we combined some of the basic concepts of stabilisation from our yachting experience, and came up with the T-foil. It operates on the same principle as the flaps on an airplane wing. When they hit turbulence, a computer-controlled stabiliser continuously adjusts to compensate for wave motion. The next step for us is to assess wave geometry and translate that information relative to the speed of the boat. A computer can then adjust the boat before it hits the wave, using less speed and power. Needless to say, this isn't the kind of device you would find on a conventional steel ship. (Harvard Business School Case Study N9-600-149, 16 August 2000, p. 13)

But, as with other Incat inventions, nobody patented the idea on the assumption that no other ship-builder could catch up.

Condor 10 also demonstrated the flexibility of these craft to the world's ferry operators. She started her operating life in 1993 on the Weymouth to Guernsey/Jersey run but switched the following year to the Cook Strait crossing in New Zealand. By 1995, she was back in the northern hemisphere plying between Helsinki and Tallinn. For the next three years, she returned to New Zealand for the southern summers, so she ran up no fewer than eight trans-ocean redelivery voyages of 12 000 nautical miles and, by 1998, had experienced no winters at all for those six years. She was the precise opposite of the itinerant ski instructor who never sees the summer.

Stena Line's *Sea Lynx I*, launched in February 1993, was the first craft to be fitted with the new marine evacuation system from one of Incat's satellite suppliers on the Hobart site—Liferaft Systems

Australia—a company created in 1992 by Robert Clifford for just this purpose. The company is still chaired by Clifford but it is owned by a network of Hobart interests (including Kim and Craig Clifford). In 1992, Clifford had become tired of buying what seemed to him to be inferior life-raft systems from a dominant supplier in Belfast. The system they devised allows one minimally trained crew member to launch the device—which resembles a fast-expanding, all-inflatable bouncy castle, complete with a covered evacuation slide to deliver passengers directly into a large roofed life-raft.

Within four minutes, a hundred evacuees can be settled in the snug interior of each raft. The system obeys the Incat dictum: it is fast, it works brilliantly and it is lightweight. And, if the navies of the world ever overcome their predilection for sailors jumping from stricken vessels into the sea, the prospects for the firm are huge. In October 2008, the Royal Navy established a precedent by ordering a A$7 million marine evacuation system for its two new aircraft carriers—HMS *Queen Elizabeth* and HMS *Prince of Wales*. Liferaft Systems Australia had supplied smaller scale systems to the navies of France, the Netherlands and the United States but this was the first, and biggest, for aircraft carriers. The Liferaft Systems Australia story is one among many demonstrating the impact of a powerful innovation incubator like Incat. Once the mother ship organisation is in place, it drives innovation and world best practice in its satellite organisations. The ripples spread far and wide when just one inventor–entrepreneur like Robert Clifford gets a following wind behind him.

Like the other firms in the Incat supply chain, Liferaft Systems Australia has expanded from its Incat origins to supplying all kinds of escape systems around the world. Its Incat trade now represents only 10–15 per cent of the total business and, of course, Liferaft Systems Australia also supplies some of Incat's fiercest commercial competitors. The firm exports 95 per cent of its production. Its owners, like almost everybody else in the 'light shipbuilding cluster' are old mates from the Hobart yachting scene.

Every ship launched during this period incorporated new ideas learned from experience of operations. For example, *Juan L*, launched in June 1993, looked exactly like the other 74-metre cats to the lay observer but she had a wider vehicle deck, a new method of supporting the superstructure (which improved the ride characteristics) and she broke new ground in the luxury of her fittings—including quite a lot of appliqué gold bling. The new owners, Buquebus of Buenos Aires, envisioned a journey in *Juan L* as rather more than just a sea crossing accompanied by your car—it was to be a stylish and luxurious adventure (and in no fewer than *four* separate, carefully targeted accommodation classes), and it also offered a vast array of shopping opportunities to the traveller. And mid-way through production of the 74-metre ships, they straightened out the sides of the craft from the original 'tumble home' styling in order to squeeze in another 24 cars. At Incat, nothing stays the same for long: *kaizen* (continuous improvement) is the name of the game.

30

Livening up the story

Altogether the company built nine of the 74-metre fast cats and the market swallowed them up as fast as the yard could make them. They had created an entirely new market for a new kind of ship and they were enjoying the fruits of meeting the market requirement. The Incat/Clifford story (as Robert McKee, the story doctor, might argue) now lacked dramatic tension—things were going too smoothly and it needed something bad or tricky to happen in order to heighten tension and expose the hero to risk. Also, the good people of Hobart had a reasonable expectation of their favourite swashbuckler. Perhaps (the scriptwriter might argue) the story needed new kinds of bigger and faster ships to test their mettle; or maybe a blockbuster courtroom drama with the old antagonist James Sherwood; or perhaps an epic yacht race in parallel; or even another grounding on the rocks of the Derwent, only much more spectacular this time (no, that would be a plot-twist too far).

Long before the construction of the last 74-metre craft they were at work on a 78-metre wave-piercer to accommodate many more people (600) and cars (150). Every increase in waterline length improved each vessel's seakeeping properties. Stena Line's *Sea Lynx II* was the first of these to set sail (in February 1994). The extra size allowed for the installation of an additional mezzanine car deck connected to the main car deck by hydraulically operated ramps. But contracting to build the ship for the Stena Line was tricky because the litigious James Sherwood was already trying to stop Stena operating an earlier ship, hull 031, on the Irish Sea crossing. She had been sold to Buquebus in South America in June 1993 and subsequently chartered by them to Stena Line. Sherwood's pound of flesh for the earlier partnership with Incat was a commercial agreement not to compete with wave-piercers within 100 miles of its own operations. As it happens, Sherwood's Sea Containers' nearest route was exactly 100 miles from Stena's but they claimed that Incat ought not to have sold to Buquebus in South America.

The case dragged its way through the courts, slowing down the development of the new bigger ships because the courts imposed restraints in the interim period. The case became one of those *Jarndyce v Jarndyce* marathons in which Sherwood claimed the separation was 99.9 miles and Stena/Incat that it was 100.1 miles, and much legal argument was devoted to the definition of 100 miles as sea passage miles or crow's flight. It was just as well Incat had an experienced lawyer on its board in the shape of Craig Clifford. In the end, the argument fetched up in the High Court of Australia (16 years later) with total victory for Incat—all the claims against the company were dismissed.

There were plenty of people who foresaw the breakdown of relations between Clifford and Sherwood; the litigation represented a sad end to a boisterous but creative partnership. Now the original trio had gone their separate ways: James Sherwood back to the labyrinthine complexities of Sea Containers' many businesses (and eventually to bankruptcy); Philip Hercus to the pure simplicities of a marine design business; and Robert Clifford, who just wanted to get on with devising and building exciting new ships. But history will show that it took the three of them in harness to make the innovative wave-piercer happen.

Meanwhile, one of Incat's best customers—South America's Buquebus company—had the idea that a really fast passenger and car-carrying ferry would be ideal for some of their protected coastal routes where rough seas are not a problem. The resultant project for a pure catamaran (no central bow for dealing with big waves) was posited on a lightship speed of 60 knots (that's 436 people and 60-plus cars speeding over the water at just under 110 kilometres per hour). Only the limitations of the available diesel horsepower reduced their target to 55 knots so the new design was dubbed the K55. Launched as *Juan Patricio* at the end of 1994, the first of this new type of craft went straight into service on the Buenos Aires to Montevideo and Colonia del Sacramento run. She is still there, zooming across the River Plate estuary, linking Argentina to Uruguay in under an hour. A somewhat bigger sister ship was built the following year for South Korea. She is also still hard at work for the Dae A Gosok company, zooming likewise between Pohang and Ulung Island and is still the fastest car/passenger ferry in the world.

So, 1994 started out interesting: two new ship types and a courtroom battle. Then it got really interesting. The ex-Premier of Tasmania Ray Groom vaguely remembers an animated conversation with Robert Clifford at a government reception in early 1994. The gist was that the fiftieth anniversary Sydney–Hobart yacht race would be setting off from Sydney Harbour on Boxing Day and it was quite wrong that the race had never been won by a yacht from the host city—Hobart. The State of Tasmania, Clifford argued, ought to support a 'decent yacht' to win the anniversary race. It wasn't a sentiment with which the Premier could possibly disagree, so he expressed a kind of general assent to the notion.

Premier Ray Groom ought to have known by then that Robert Clifford has an imperfectly developed sense of what is not possible. If something is obviously sensible, you just do it and the Lord or some other powerful agency (the Tasmanian Government, for example) will provide. Clifford the first-born had known that since he was about seven. The Premier was no stranger to Incat; indeed he was their local MP. Some months before, he had been persuaded to spend a few hours getting to know the business better. Like most VIP guests he had been picked up by the boss in the youngest of his Rolls-Royce originated motor cars (the 1987 long-wheelbase Bentley Turbo R, since you ask) and taken for a spin in a big cat. He remembers it well, especially the nerve-racking moment when the boss instructed: 'Go on—you have a steer, Ray!'

A few weeks later, the Premier got a phone call out of the blue from a dockside in Southampton: 'I've got the boat!'—the boat being the 26-metre Bruce Farr designed maxi-ketch *New Zealand Endeavour*, which was available for short-term charter, having just won the Whitbread around-the-world race. Robert Clifford had succeeded in snatching the yacht from under the noses of a much better connected syndicate involving David Kellett (over 30 Sydney–Hobart races and skipper of the only Australian boat at that time to combine line honours in the race with the handicap trophy), the haircare magnate Anton Starling, and the hugely experienced Jack Goluzd (27 Sydney–Hobarts). Poor Goluzd, thanks to Robert Clifford, ended up crewing on Tony Paolo's *Condor of Currabubula* which came in 10th.

Everybody knew from *New Zealand Endeavour*'s showing in the 1992 race that she was the right boat for the job—but Clifford got in first. Perhaps that explains Clifford's use of the definite article in his phone call to Premier Groom—not 'I've got *a* boat' but 'I've got *the* boat'. Clifford aspired to winning the Sydney–Hobart at some point, so the fiftieth race, the association with Ray Groom and the chance to plug his home state simply provided the pretext. All that was required of the Premier was to authorise the government to take on the project immediately, foot most of the bill and leave it to Robert Clifford to skipper the boat (renamed *Tasmania*) to victory in the fiftieth race. The Premier, of course, had only the vaguest recollection of the original conversation, and now he found himself taking instruction as to a major Tasmanian promotional project. The thing is it was a good idea (provided they won the race), and as it happened Incat had the wherewithal to make it happen: Kerry Sturmey to manage the project, a crew of Incat sailors and, of course, a skipper.

The Tasmanian Government ended up sponsoring a portion of the project costs in order to secure the naming rights, but the only practical way to get the yacht quickly from Southampton (the Whitbread finishing place) to Hobart was for Robert Clifford and two collaborators to buy it (for US$425 000). This they did, only selling the boat in late 1995 after a year's further racing and 'fun'. By September, the renamed *Tasmania* had arrived in Melbourne ready for fitting out and crew selection and training. The call went out for experienced crew—in the yachting world this is mostly a word-of-mouth process—and crew trials began in September.

It was always understood that the nucleus of the crew would be made up of Incat people: in practice, a roll-call of the nicknames—Frizzle (Graeme Freeman) as sailing master, Rowdy (Stephen McCullum) as principal rigger, and the rest of the crew were Stringbean (Craig Clifford), Hanger (John Harris, soon to be a director of the firm), Curly (David Stalker), Lightning (Richard Boult), Sludge (Michael Cooper) and others. Nick Wells, one of the early members of the Incat technical management team and latterly head of the US military operations, was also a crew member; no one seems to know why he lacks a Tasmanian nickname (although he is reported to be known as 'The Lump' by his American colleagues). Of course, Beanhead (Robert Clifford) was the skipper. A sociologist could probably explain the importance of obligatory nicknames in this yachting subculture. Kerry Sturmey, without a nickname being a mere woman, ran the project—from arranging further commercial sponsorship, through managing the finances, to mother-henning the crews: scheduling and provisioning the training weekends, kitting the 24 crew members out in a range of themed uniforms, including 'two heads, two masts' T-shirts (a not-so-subtle reference to mainstream Australia's scurrilous view that all Tasmanians are in-bred) and, for the race itself, Incat welding shirts.

October 1994 turned out to be the most dramatic month in a very eventful year. But, just at the end of September, another of Robert Clifford's prophetic hunches was tragically vindicated. For years he had been trying to dampen the operators' appetite for bow doors in ferries, arguing that they were time-consuming to fit, they required continual maintenance and they added weight (the worst sin of all) and cost. Really, his main objection was that bow doors represented an outmoded and inelegant design solution to the problem of loading and unloading vehicles, especially as the bigger Incat vessels now had room for a system of ramps—after the fashion of a city car park. And, of course, the presence of the bow door weakened the integrity of the entire structure. Then, on 28 September, the Finnish-registered *Estonia* went down in the Baltic Sea en route from Tallinn to Stockholm with the loss of 852 lives—fatally weakened by a failed bow door. In a conventional monohull, bow door failures result in an inrush of water that is sudden and catastrophic—the 15 000 tonne *Estonia* went down in about 35 minutes.

As it happens, an Incat bow door failure would not have admitted water to hull spaces, but the *Estonia* gave Clifford the ammunition he needed. *Cat-Link I*, completed the following year, was the last Incat craft to be built with a bow door. But Clifford acknowledges that the purist approach to design contradicted the 'market-led' philosophy taught in the business schools:

I know we lost sales to Austal [Incat's fiercest competitor in Western Australia] because they were willing to give the customer a ship with a bow door, but I'm convinced it's contrary to what the customer really needs . . . one lane out the front just isn't as good as four out the back. We can almost always convince the customers that it is in their best interests but there are occasions when they just don't understand their own business.

This is not a statement calculated to get you high marks in any 'marketing' exam.

31

Another fine mess

Meanwhile, despite the court proceedings with Sherwood, Incat had contracted with Holyman Ferries to build another 78-metre cat, signing the contract in June 1994. She was to be named *Condor 11*. Construction proceeded at the usual swift pace and the vessel was ready for her sea trials by the end of September. On 3 September, they announced the names of the crew for the Sydney–Hobart race. Then, Robert Clifford's role as local legend was cemented by what happened on 8 October—firstly, the formal announcement at noon of the Sydney–Hobart challenge and then, just nine hours later at 9.00 pm, *another* grounding on the rocks of the Derwent, but this time a great deal more spectacular.

Robert was at the helm as usual and they were going very fast—about 40 knots. On board were 48 people, including many from Holymans, the new owners. A combination of radar malfunction and navigational error had taken them straight onto the Black Jack Reef near the entrance to the river—a semi-submerged geological feature well known to all Hobart's sailors. It took the ship a full boat-length to come to a stop, by which time the port hull had lifted six metres vertically and so was about a metre and a half clear of the water surface. The starboard hull lifted only three metres, barely clear of the water. Many on board were hurled into bulkheads and one was knocked unconscious—not surprising as the craft had decelerated from about 70 kilometres per hour to standstill in the space of 90 metres. Rough weather prevented an immediate rescue so everybody was obliged to bed down for the night. It wasn't what you would call an ideal proving trial. There was a hurried discussion that night on the best PR approach; the conclusion being that Robert Clifford should assemble all the workforce the following morning and confess ('We fucked up!'), and then make a public pronouncement of culpability ('The buck stops here.'). Something had to be said; the grounding actually made the front page of *The Times* in London.

It was obvious the boat would not be easy to shift. It was largely high and dry and it weighed about 700 tonnes. That was the bad news. The sliver of good news was the craft's survival capacity had proved itself yet again. Of the 16 watertight compartments, six were completely undamaged. The main problem was how to get the ship off the reef without causing further damage. It took 42 days of trial and error to achieve that. During that time, Incat and Robert Clifford reclaimed their place in the state's headlines. The local newspapers reported the unfolding story day after day with undisguised glee, speculating wildly about the true causes of the accident and prognosticating gloomily about the likely outcomes. In a small town like Hobart, there isn't a lot of bona fide news, as such, so a 'character' like Robert Clifford is always a gift to popular journalism; all this happened at the birth of 'celebrity culture'. *Condor 11* became showbiz.

As if on cue, the Premier's Awards for Export Success were scheduled for the period of *Condor 11*'s unwelcome elevation. In presenting the award to Incat, Premier Ray Groom (having barely survived the pressure to fund the Sydney–Hobart adventure) commented: 'Someone suggested we should put a parking meter down there to get some revenue but I think that's a bit unkind!'

Meanwhile, back on the reef, most of the effort (having repaired some of the damaged compartments on the spot) went into tugging the vessel backwards off the rocks using no fewer than five 22 000 horsepower tugs plus, eventually, the commandeered French Antarctic icebreaker *L'Astrolabe*. The show was watched, day after day, by a flotilla of up to 50 ferries, pleasure craft, fishing boats and even jet-skis—not to mention hundreds of people gathered on the foreshore of Goat Bluff, including a semi-permanent Mr Whippy. It became Hobart's big day out with the kids.

Once the attempt to build a slipway under the craft failed, because of a stubborn outcrop of rock, the solution lay in the creation of 'the biggest hovercraft in the world' to virtually float it off on a cushion of air on 20 November. This meant concreting over holes in the engine room floor, employing a couple of 500-tonne hydraulic jacks and compressing air into the damaged floats until the vessel got back home. As Robert Clifford points out, it's not likely anybody else will have exactly the same problem but, if anybody does, 'I now know exactly what to do!' He never lacked for advice during the emergency—receiving an average of 200 letters every day with helpful suggestions for shifting the boat (most, but not all, crackpot). Somebody helpfully suggested hiring a squad of Russian super-helicopters to uplift the whole vessel. Hobart certainly felt involved with the problem; this was their favourite son in a bit of bother yet again.

It was an expensive exercise and it put back delivery of *Condor 11* by about two months. But it did prove the durability of these ships and the fast ferry world took note accordingly. The survey authorities took various measurements and concluded they could relax a number of building constraints as a result. Incat still claims to be the only ferry-maker to have undergone the Volvo Crash Test—and challenges other ship-builders to match their achievement. The good folk of Hobart got an exciting 42-day entertainment with the central actor (the chief executive) heroically directing operations from the bridge of the stranded vessel. Robert

McKee would have approved—things had been going too smoothly in recent times. *Condor 11* (hull 034) was duly delivered to Holyman Ferries on 2 April 1995—after a Herculean catch-up effort. The delivery voyage to Weymouth took a month. Meanwhile, *Cat-Link I* was being constructed in parallel in the new bigger 'Coverdales' shed next door.

32

The sailor hero

In November and December of that eventful year, the Sydney–Hobart challenge was developing in parallel. The team didn't have long to get *Tasmania* and her newly selected crew ready for the big race, and the boss (and skipper) was severely distracted by the events on Black Jack Reef. But they got a bit of practice sailing the boat from Geelong to Hobart at the end of her delivery voyage from Southampton, as well as some practice in refloating the yacht after running aground (you couldn't make it up!). Every weekend from then on was devoted to serious race preparation. The boss was forced to miss the two-day Maria Island race in mid-November, but they won it just the same and in record time. After all, he had assembled a first-rate crew. 'Frizzle' Freeman the sailing master was virtually a professional sailor and the rest of the non-Incat crew were some of Tasmania's finest. By the time the big race came around they were throwing the enormous maxi around like a dinghy.

Some of the swankier New South Wales crews assumed a Tasmanian entry (even on the established *New Zealand Endeavour*) would be a touch amateurish. This impression may have been reinforced by the enthusiastic partying night after night of the Tasmanian crew and by the presence of agricultural characters like the boat's 'sewerman', Harold '4.30' Bain (a shearer by trade whose nickname reflected the time he usually got home from parties). The sewerman's job was to lurk in the bowels of the yacht untangling and parcelling up the wet and heavy sails thrown down the hatch by the crew. It took about five crewmen on deck to manhandle a single sail; '4.30' managed them on his own without complaint and, apparently, without difficulty (shearers tend to have hands the size of dinner plates). The reader can intuit the contrast with the kinds of fair-weather sailors on some of the plusher Sydney-based boats, many of whom were probably getting to bed on time in anticipation of the great contest to come. Not the Tasmanians. But they went on practising—once they finally woke up in the mornings. Meanwhile, there was *Juan Patricio*, the first of the very fast K-class ferries to be launched (on 4 December) and the delayed fitout of *Condor 11* and *Cat-Link I* to be managed in parallel.

The last fortnight of December was given over to a series of yacht races and 21 to 23 December to the sponsors' promotional usage of the boat including, of course, the main sponsor, the State of Tasmania. En route to Sydney they had had the chance to try out the last of the enormous stock of sails that had come with the purchase of the boat. The race itself wasn't quite a cakewalk. For a start, there were a record 371 yachts entered for the fiftieth anniversary race, the largest fleet ever, including many of the biggest and fastest sailing boats in the world. And the Sydney–Hobart race is always challenging and sometimes very dangerous. This is because the route takes the contestants through a sea passage where wind nearly always battles current. Once the boats leave the relative protection of the New South Wales coast for the crossing to Tasmania, they are exposed to southwesterly storms which blow up from the Antarctic. Because Bass Strait is so shallow, the effect of storms on wind versus current can lead to wildly unpredictable seas.

Tasmania was first out of Sydney Heads, but fell back to second and third in the strong southeast headwinds that took them down the coast. They encountered ideal east to northeast winds over Bass Strait and, when a strong southwest wind roared in as they approached Tasmania, the maxi took off at about 18 knots. The rest of the fleet were battered by the southwesterly and some 40 boats had to scuttle into Eden on the New South Wales south coast for safety. Meanwhile, up front, Robert Clifford was certain they were well clear of the fleet by then but, battling across Storm Bay in a 50 knot headwind, a light suddenly appeared not far behind them at about 3.00 am on 28 December. It turned out to be George Snow's *Brindabella* bearing down on them and handling the headwind rather better than *Tasmania*.

If Robert Clifford knew it was *Brindabella*, he kept the news to himself; either because of a refusal to acknowledge a real threat, or to keep up the spirits of his crew. This is a recurrent theme in the Clifford saga: it's hard to know for sure whether the man simply fails to register the presence of obstacles, or he takes note but decides to ignore them on behalf of his flock, or he engages fully with stark reality but trusts to luck. *Tasmania*'s predicament in Storm Bay on 28 December 1994 subsequently became Incat's predicament in 2002 when bankruptcy threatened the company. On that occasion, no one really knew whether the skipper was piloting the Incat craft on the basis of wilful ignorance, pride or absolute faith in providence.

As it happens, *Brindabella* was one of the Sydney–Hobart race's most respected regulars and is still holder of a number of Australia's sailing speed records—including at that time the fastest Sydney–Hobart with conventional ballast—but this particular *Brindabella* had never won the race. So at the end it was a cliff-hanger; *Tasmania* got over the line at about 6.30 am just five minutes ahead, courtesy of just one tactical mistake by *Brindabella*. After two and a half days' racing, that was too close for comfort. They had done it, for the honour of Australia's island state, for the promotion of Incat the ship-builder and for the greater glory of Robert Clifford, now aged a dignified 51 years of age. The celebrations in Hobart that night, and for a few days after, have achieved legendary status in a town that likes a celebratory drink or two.

George Snow got his revenge a few months afterwards when *Brindabella* beat *Tasmania* in the annual Sydney to Mooloolaba race. The celebrations that night cost George Snow and Robert Clifford quite a lot of money; the problem being that the two crews occupied opposite sides of the same restaurant, which meant, naturally, an epic food-fight and a massive damages bill to the restaurateur. That's how it is with sailing folk. George Snow and *Brindabella* finally won the Sydney–Hobart race three years later, which is as it should be.

Just to make life interesting and challenging, 1994 also marked Incat's embarkation on a further step-change in the capacity of the fast ferry—without ever compromising on speed. In theory, it was all incremental development; in practice, they were pushing against design limits. The last 74-metre ship was built in 1993. Over the course of the next five years, they increased the overall length to 78 metres, then 81 metres, then 86 metres, then 91 metres, then 96 metres, then 98 metres. In those five years, they had doubled passenger capacity from 450 to 900, tripled car capacity from 84 to 260 or up to 330 truck lane metres (about 16 trucks and trailers), and all without sacrifice of the ships' not-so-secret weapon—speed. Hull 046, the first of the 91-metre cats, actually achieved an incredible 50 knots lightship speed during her trials. More important still, they managed to increase deadweight capacity (what you can carry, as opposed to the weight of the ship itself) fourfold from just under 200 tonnes to 800 tonnes. By the time they got to 96 metres, they had constructed the first fast ship in the world capable of carrying a greater deadweight tonnage than its own lightship tonnage at high speed. Of course, if you're not in a hurry or you want to economise on fuel, you can carry even more.

Crucially, the increased size of the vessels brought accompanying advances in flexibility for the operator. Right from the start, Clifford (one step ahead of the market as usual) had understood that the very fast cat would need eventually to carry heavy freight loads and big trucks. Most of the owners were conservative and thus were over-focused on passenger traffic. So the first 'highway mix' ship (hull 050) was late on the scene, but from then on most of the main customers' businesses were transformed. Because all the latest designs incorporated hydraulically hoistable decks and ramps, the operators can adjust their load plans quickly to accommodate different traffic mixes and daily sailing fluctuations. And, to take advantage of 'shoulder' seasons and night freight runs, they can raise the mezzanine decks to deck-head level to squeeze in the maximum number of freight vehicles. The big fast cat had become a bit like one of those family 'multi-purpose vehicles' on the roads—adaptable to almost any purpose. Robert Clifford, it is important to remember, is an ex-ferryman—an operator, not just a boat-builder.

33

A family business

Kim Clifford got married to Richard Lowrie (then Incat's sales and marketing manager) on 11 March 1995. The plan was for a typical grandstanding event, taking place at sea on board the newly built *Cat-Link I*, supported by Robert's vintage Rolls-Royces on land. Except that when the bride-to-be arrived from Melbourne two days beforehand, it turned out that (despite Robert's over-optimistic predictions) the ship wasn't going anywhere. It had no engines and no stern at all—a victim of the *Condor 11* delays. So Kim got married in the Coverdales yard instead, but still on board the ship. The wedding motorcade (two of the vintage Rolls-Royces and the follow-up Bentley for emergencies) got as far as the top of the boatyard road before the 1926 20/25 horsepower Rolls-Royce, piloted by the father of the bride, lost all its electrics. With the bride-to-be in the back, the driver leaped out, stripped to shirtsleeves, and dived into the engine to fix the problem. Meanwhile, the following Roller, Craig at the wheel, started to overheat, so he didn't dare turn off the engine, reasoning that one vintage Rolls-Royce abandoned by the side of the road might be a bit embarrassing but two would be very embarrassing indeed,

139

especially as most of the wedding party would have to run to the big event. He drove on.

Kim was phlegmatic about the whole thing. She had learned long since that her father's extravagant plans sometimes went awry but nothing was ever dull. As Craig reflected afterwards: 'I think she learned that . . . if there is a safe, risk-free way of doing things it is unlikely to attract his attention . . . why do something the easy way when the challenging way is much more of an adventure!' At this stage of her life, Kim was still thinking in terms of a separate (non-Incat) existence, but her wedding was a very Incat sort of event—lots of swash and buckle with a bit of prudent emergency response built in, just in case—but all in the family (the Incat family).

Kim's wedding, emergencies and all, should have forewarned her she was doomed to an Incat future. After all, she had been in the public eye launching ships all her life, including the *James McCabe* at the age of five and the much grander *Our Lady Pamela* (hull 021) at 17. Within two years of her wedding, she became a director of the firm. It could have been worse. Later Kim would reflect:

He [Robert] pushed hard for his children to be part of the business, with both Craig and I resisting for some time. The timing was right for me to return to Hobart as I was pregnant with my first child. I can remember taking time to adjust to being a new mum when Robert rocked up to the house and his only [characteristically tactful] offer of support was: 'Don't worry, your mother wasn't very good at it at the start either!' [Barbara, remember, was bringing up the infants Craig and Kim at the time, mostly on board boats and simultaneously cooking for a flotilla of itinerant fishermen.] He was not contented until I was back at work—and I guess he was right—I was a better mother with aspirations outside the home. Robert did, and still does, put his business aspirations before everyday family matters. That is simply how it is. I have always known that and bear no grudges for it as he comes with many other attributes. (correspondence, 2008)

Robert Clifford's younger brother Tony was subject to the same kind of suasion—beginning with Robert's aborted enterprise to build a 'Black Soo' yacht in the backyard of the family home in 1961. At the time. Tony was 12 and the big brother 'stand-over merchant' 18. Predictably, the slave labour was whipped in on the premise: 'If you don't help me [with construction] I will never take you out sailing in it.' That about sums it up. Tony managed to make a substantial career outside the growing family firm, although he spent 15 years back in the fold, but Anne Clifford, the middle child, made her escape to the mainland.

On reflection, Craig and Kim Clifford's upbringing was really rather like their great-grandfather Elijah Clifford's boyhood in inner-London Clerkenwell, where all family members were recruited to the central cause in a flourishing manufactory. That is how it was for most people before the tyranny of distant and incomprehensible big company employment work took fathers away from their children and doomed many mothers to solitary household drudgery. Robert Clifford's children had an unusual upbringing in twentieth century Hobart terms, but not in the longer logic of history. They grew up in the shadow of a great enterprise, and under the sway of a *paterfamilias* figure, which seemed to them to be the most natural thing in the world.

34

Technology, leadership and example

It is easy to make the argument that sailors, as a breed, are equipped with extra-special intellectual powers because they are always dealing with complexity, and thus calculating as they go. They compute the interaction of their particular craft with fluky winds, infinitely variable water conditions and they take decisions continuously, based on assumptions about possible futures. It is all much more complex than banking, or doctoring, or most other professional callings. We know from sad experience that a surprising number of group-thinking businessmen can come to believe they can dictate the terms of external reality. That was Enron's big mistake—believing they could invent and then control a completely new 'market'. That was the big mistake of all the bankers who persuaded themselves that 'derivative' financial products had the power to control risk in the real world. No sailor ever does anything like this. If the sailor is inventive, he will be impelled to innovate when it comes to gear and equipment. And all sailors copy good ideas from other sailors. That is pretty much the story of Incat and of all the part-time and semi-professional sailors who have made up the Incat family over the years. J.P. Morgan, the famous New

York banker, once said: 'I'll do business with anyone, but I'll only go sailing with gentlemen.'

So when Robert Clifford heard about the inauguration of an international solar-powered boat race to be held on Lake Burley Griffin in Canberra in April of 1996, it was obvious that Incat should develop a boat for it and, of course, win it. To do so he had to assemble a team of volunteer designers, electronic engineers and naval architects from the Incat family and to divert something like 2000 man hours to the project. All that the volunteers lacked was any specialist knowledge at all of solar power. That, in a way, was the fun of it. They came up with a 6-metre catamaran (of course) built for one supine man suspended in a kind of pod between the two hulls. A horserace jockey might have been the ideal pilot, but the substantially heavier Robert Clifford took command for most of the race. The maker of the hulls, a local shipwright Gordon Stewart, subsequently joined the Incat family in the design team. The craft was equipped with a tiltable 'sail' entirely festooned with solar panels, designed to be aimed at the sun and all connected to a bank of batteries and a small electric outboard motor. Incat won the race easily. It was conducted over six hours in an anti-clockwise direction around the lake. Incat hull 039 achieved both fastest lap (3.11 nautical miles at 9.76 knots) and the longest distance travelled (34.41 nautical miles) at an average speed of just over 6 knots.

So far as the diffusion of innovation is concerned, the point of this story is that among the crowd watching the race was a young (37-year-old) sailing fanatic (accompanied by his two sons), who practised as a general practitioner in the seaside town of Ulladulla on the New South Wales south coast. Dr Robert Dane was the kind of man who would devote five family holidays on the trot to wavesailing in Hawaii. This, after all, is a tale about sailors. Dane found himself intrigued by the difficulty Robert Clifford had in controlling the craft when the wind got up. It wasn't designed as a sailboat, merely as a receptacle for solar energy, but it clearly *wanted* to sail. Clifford was obliged sometimes to fix the sail in the horizontal in order to stay upright. Some of the other contestants had to remove their panels because of the wind. Dane immediately saw the potential of a hybrid vessel deriving its energy both from the sun and the wind.

That was his 'crystallising moment' (remember Howard Gardner's insight about observation causing reading; back in the mid-1950s Robert Clifford started to read only when he knew he had something very important to learn). Robert Dane got to reading about wings and made the discovery that the evolution of insects started with the emergence of little buds for collecting solar energy, which evolved in the end into proper wings for flying. In other words, there was a precedent in nature for the evolution of a solar/sail hybrid craft. Dane turned 38 in September 1996, and promptly sold his medical practice (in December) in order to concentrate on building a boat to win the next year's race. Which he duly did with the *Marjorie K*, defeating 40 international competitors by achieving 6 knots on wind power alone and 12–15 knots when power was transferred to the motor.

So in 1996, Robert Dane was sparked by an Incat design in just the same way as Robert Clifford was triggered by Christopher Cockerill's hovercraft 20 years before. At 37, Dane was near enough the same age too. With the Canberra race under his belt, Dane set about assembling a team of enthusiasts to make 'Solar Sailor' commercially viable. That team included Bruce Heggie (the renowned surfboard maker) and Max Hayward (an ex-British Aerospace engineer). The result—the first Solar Sailor—can be seen and travelled on by tourists and technology nuts alike in Sydney. It is the first sun-and-wind-powered passenger boat in commercial use, and it carries 100 people at up to 15 knots on solar and wind power alone. It uses solar panels on its deck to capture sunlight and also on its multiple wings, which are pivotally mounted at their bases (not unlike an insect's wings) in order to permit computer-controlled multi-plane movement to maximise sun and wind conditions—or to fold flat (just like an insect's wings) if it gets too windy. In reserve is a chargeable battery and a gas-powered engine for emergencies.

He set up Solar Sailor Holdings Ltd in 1999. Then he persuaded Bob Hawke, Australia's ex-Prime Minister, to serve on the board as chairman of the new company to develop and exploit the new technology. It is a very good example of the way that genuinely creative people build on the genius of other people. Everyone knows the quote attributed to Sir Isaac Newton: 'If I have seen a little further than others, it is by standing on the shoulders of giants', which means there can be no such thing as entirely 'original' work, we all pay attention to the work of our predecessors. The great sixteenth century Danish astronomer Tycho Brahe observed the heavens obsessively for year upon year so that his young assistant Kepler, standing on Brahe's shoulders, was enabled to set out the basic laws of planetary motion. Newton acknowledged his debt to them both. And, with Clifford and Dane in mind, many, but not all, inventors are also entrepreneurs: Thomas Alva Edison being a famous example of the type. But they seem to be inventors first and entrepreneurs by extension. Maybe Dane would have made his breakthrough (from medicine to his life's work) without the example of Robert Clifford. But maybe not. Maybe Robert Clifford would have come upon his life's work without the exposure to sailing while at Hutchins School. But maybe not.

In parallel with Dane, Robert Clifford the inventor was already at work on 'the wing'—an experimental craft designed to travel on water at sufficient speed to achieve partial liftoff in a controllable way. If it can be achieved in scale, the craft promises a way of transporting very large cargoes with very much reduced frictional force; that is, using the physics of aeronautics to overcome the physics of seagoing. Before the very fast aluminium wave-piercing catamaran entered the stage, carrying people and goods on the sea meant very heavy steel ships pushing lots of water out of the way and consuming enormous amounts of fuel oil in the process. The fast wave-piercer has to shift very much less water to achieve similar payloads because it is so much lighter overall (so it sinks into the water less) and so much 'skinnier' through the water. The wing simply takes the quest to the next level of efficiency. Like Robert Dane—another sailor—Clifford wants to harness wind power but this time utilising aeroplane-like speed to achieve lift.

As with all the Clifford models and prototypes, the wing has been through many iterations in the process of testing. It started as a simple half-metre paper dart to test out its 'ground effect' properties. The next was a heavier craft of about one metre which was powered and revolved like a model aircraft on a string. Then followed a series of 7–10-metre craft powered by outboard motor. The most successful test flight (from the technical standpoint) dumped Clifford in the bay at about 50 knots when it achieved just a bit too much lift and flipped over completely. This was, however, a success because it showed how the vessel's resistance lowered as it lifted out of the water; unfortunately, the outboards continued to power the craft forward. He landed, severely bruised, about 50 metres short of where the craft came down. The only unbruised area on his body was the white imprint on his backside where his wallet had been. On the way to casualty, he already knew what to do next—design a means of reducing forward thrust in near-liftoff.

The current prototype 'wing' vessel can be seen from time to time zooming around Hobart, gathering operational data. The current version weighs 3.5 tonnes and carries just two people. The challenge now is to provide a power source which will automatically reduce thrust and fuel consumption to achieve a controllable 90 per cent airborne passage. In the longer run, the possibility is for the carriage of 200 people and their cars at 70 knots (around 130 kilometres per hour) over inshore waters, at which point the craft begins to offer serious competition to aircraft. Everything will be carried in the wing structure, supported by three floats and propelled either by surface-piercing props or a self-regulating high-speed paddle (as the craft rises, the paddle's impact diminishes). The main windows can be located in the leading edge of the wing. Later still, it should be possible to build a large-scale freight version to shift goods across the sea at high speed using about one-quarter of the power required today. It is the logical next step for an inventor engaged in a lifelong engagement with the elements in the service of transportation.

Every few years, a new type of craft finds its way into the Incat roster. The hull numbers tell the story. Hull number 013 was *Little Devil*—the prototype of the first wave-piercer, launched in 1984—and the practical experiment that launched the entire wave-piercing, fast ferry revolution. Hull number 039 was the solar sail from 1996 that effectively launched Robert Dane's breakthrough with 'solar sailor'. The wing (hull 054) appeared on the scene in 1999, so the interested observer would expect a new experimental craft to appear around about 2006. And so it did. This latest experimental craft (hull 063) is a small 17-metre propeller-driven, fast (33 knots) cat suitable for multiple commercial and 'live-aboard' pleasure uses. Its experimental usefulness to Incat lies in the super-streamlined mode of production, rather than its technical features as such. This means that a small production line could easily churn out one ship a week with all the metalwork complete and engines installed, so that a retailer or user can customise the craft for multiple uses—from 'gin palaces' to police, customs and military use.

With experimental hull 063, Robert Clifford is returning to a tried-and-tested Incat principle that the way you make them may be as important commercially as what you make. This distinction was at the bottom of the split from the designer Philip Hercus in 1988; Clifford understood that the manufacturing process itself was an Incat USP (unique selling proposition). The most obvious example of this insight was the Clifford imitation of the Boeing modus operandi—making a craft to a standard 'sea frame' for customisation by the client later on. But there is an earlier precursor in Robert Clifford's love of the Rolls-Royce marque. Once Henry Royce more-or-less perfected the manufacturing process which produced the Rolls-Royce car's uncanny smoothness and quietness, he started handing over the finishing and customisation to a range of established coachbuilders. As it happens, Robert Clifford's most ancient Rolls-Royces, from 1923 and 1926, have retro-fitted Australian coachwork but the younger cars, the Phantom II from 1933 and the 1935 vehicle, have bodies lovingly constructed at the time of manufacture by Messrs H.J. Mulliner & Co. and Thrupp & Maberley (coachbuilders to Her Majesty the Queen).

Role models generally play an important part in the formation of unusual or outstanding people. Fred Clifford and Jack Newman (the first 'boss') aside, probably the most influential figure for Robert Clifford, once he was old enough to understand such matters, was Henry Royce. Clifford is a serious student of the history of the Rolls-Royce company and of the founding partnership that built it. Rolls and Royce worked so well together because of their complementarity. Royce was the not-so-posh engineering and manufacturing genius and Rolls was the very posh salesman. The peculiarity of Incat is that its founder was both the builder and the not-so-posh salesman. Put Rolls and Royce together and you get genius.

It is tempting to see Royce the engineer and manufacturer as the true inspiration for Robert Clifford, but it's not that simple. The Honourable Charles Rolls, the well-connected entrepreneur, also had a degree in mechanical engineering from Cambridge and spent much of his life trying out daredevil contraptions, just like Clifford. He was the second Briton to be licensed to fly an aircraft, having befriended the Wright brothers. That's how he killed himself—at the controls of an early Flyer assembled in the Wrights' French workshop in 1910—the first Briton to die in an air crash. But it was Henry Royce who provided Robert Clifford with his template for manufacturing production: 'Strive for perfection in everything that you do. Take the best that exists and make it better. When it does not exist, design it.' Royce was a businessman of sorts but his real zeal was for perfecting the performance of the motor cars. If you build a better mousetrap . . .

35

It's not what you do; it's the way that you do it

As the millennium came to an end, big manufacturing firms all over the world increasingly outsourced their manufacturing to low-cost countries in the far east and eastern Europe. The idea was that you could hang on to your intellectual property while greatly decreasing your costs. That intellectual property was supposed to be locked up in a vast array of expensive patents. Robert Clifford, we must remember, always turned his nose up at patent protection—it was expensive and, worse still, it placed you at the mercy of lawyers. The Incat USP (unique selling proposition) was always to move faster than everyone else—in product development and market applications. That was why Clifford understood that knowing how to make the ships was more valuable than the designs themselves. After all, the ships were constantly evolving. As he put it: 'What we do have is mostly in our heads and it is a sort of IP [intellectual property] which is far more valuable than being on paper.' So it is unlikely that Clifford ever seriously considered shifting his manufacturing operations from Hobart, even though Mark Wickham (who wrote a learned PhD thesis about Incat) suggests that he wasn't above threatening the Tasmanian Government with a move interstate if he didn't get the treatment he felt the firm deserved.

By 2009, a series of research studies revealed that whenever a big firm relocated its basic manufacturing to another country, the requirement for manufacturing agility and versatility demanded the creation of a kind of information conduit between the headquarters and the manufacturing sites—a sort of evolutionary feedback loop. Increasingly (and, as the researchers demonstrated, inevitably), the locus of invention shifted to the manufacturing site. All the patents in the world could not prevent that transfer of essential knowhow and cleverness. In other words, making things makes you clever; we were, as a species, *Homo habilis* before we were *Homo sapiens*. Arguably, *Homo habilis* led inexorably to *Homo sapiens*. As the Nobel Laureate chemist Sir Harry Kroto said: 'Nobody learns things without actually doing things'; so it is not surprising that Incat itself started to attract research attention. It was the subject of another learned treatise by Australian academics entitled 'An Unconventional Approach to Intellectual Property Protection: The Case of an Australian Firm Transferring Shipbuilding Technologies to China' (McGaughey et al., *Journal of World Business*, vol. 35, issue 1, 2000, pp. 1–20).

This research also demonstrated that Clifford's difficulties with formal contracting (especially with the labyrinthine complexities of the US military) were compensated for by a facility for dealing informally with Asian businessmen. The eminent scholar Charles Hampden-Turner has written extensively about the problems western businessmen encounter when they deal with the Japanese and the Chinese, especially when circumstances surrounding contracts change (*The Seven Cultures of Capitalism*, 1993). The Harvard Business School approach is generally to stick slavishly to the legalistic wording of the contract, even if doing so may destroy both businesses. Asian businesses generally value relationships based on trust more highly than the letter of the law. If there is an important change in external circumstances, the Asian businessman is far more likely to accept or to initiate a modification to the contract. He does this because the idea of 'partnership' means more to him than squeezing contractors till the pips squeak.

Here again, Clifford was ahead of the game. Throughout the 1980s, Incat managed a licensing relationship with the AFAI Corporation of Hong Kong for production of the K-class fast ferry. This matured into a joint venture in the 1990s. Speaking of the original contract, the chairman of AFAI (another *paterfamilias* of a family firm) remarked: 'It was basically a gentleman's agreement. There was a licensing contract but we never signed it . . . you can never get the words right.' The unconventional logic of AFAI's managing director also made perfect sense to Robert Clifford: 'This is where you need to approach a different thinking. Often, if you want to honour (an agreement) you will not sign (the contract). The person who would not honour it probably would sign it.'

J.T. Li, writing in *Managing International Ventures in China*, put it: 'Although the actual process of drafting the unsigned agreement may have facilitated the development of trust and understanding, the long term relationship between Incat and AFAI appears to have been pivotal to the operations of the venture' (2001). All this would make sense to Charles Hampden-Turner. The only surprise might be that Clifford is a Tasmanian, but a Tasmanian whose word is his bond and whose judgement of trustworthiness is seldom faulty. And then, in 1988, an ex-pat Tasmanian, Jonathan West, took up a professorial post at the Harvard Business School. One of his first acts was to institute a case study based on Incat for the Harvard students. It became a staple in the world's pre-eminent business school.

36

Coasting to international success

As the end of the millennium approached, Robert Clifford moved into his late 50s and began to think about stepping up (to the chairmanship of Incat) and moving on—obviously not to retirement—but to a base closer to the main clients in Europe. In the late 1990s most of the action in the fast ferry world centred on the Baltic, the North Sea and the Mediterranean and involved customer-operators in Norway, Denmark, Germany and Spain, plus one loyal customer from Uruguay/Argentina. Moving on meant the children, Craig and Kim, stepping up to the plate because Robert Clifford's image of the firm was essentially that of a family firm. By that time he had gathered around him a very experienced and loyal team of senior managers, but he wasn't yet ready to hand over control to a professional managerial cadre. And Craig and Kim still weren't absolutely certain that running the firm by themselves was what they wanted.

All this time the ships were getting bigger and the market remained fertile. The years 1996, 1997 and 1998 had a remarkable symmetry: they produced flat out to capacity in each year (four ships per annum); the first three at last year's dimension and the last a bit bigger. At the end of 1996, they constructed the first 86-metre craft, at the end of 1997 the first 91-metre and in 1998 the first 96-metre. Hull 046 achieved a remarkable 50 knots-plus speed on her lightship trials. Then in both 1999 and 2000, Incat built three 96-metre ships; the last of them—later Brittany Ferries' *Normandie Express* at 98 metres (the bigger-still Evolution 10B design)—was launched on 24 November 1999, and almost immediately went into service as a floating exhibition ship on Sydney Harbour during the XXVIIth Olympiad. She was available for that purpose because she had not found an immediate buyer; an early warning sign of stickiness in the global fast ferry market.

Meanwhile, Incat relived former glories with not one but two new assaults on the Blue Riband—the Hales Trophy—for the fastest crossing of the Atlantic by a passenger vessel. First up was *Catalonia* (hull 047), ordered by the South American firm Buquebus—in fact the sixth fast ferry they had bought from Incat. At the last moment, Buquebus decided to shift the ship from the Argentina–Uruguay run to Spanish routes. They were impressed by the speeds they had achieved in trials—48.7 knots (lightship) and 43 knots at full load, so it looked like they might easily eclipse the average 36.966 knots for the crossing set by *Hoverspeed Great Britain* eight years before. It would be possible to make the last leg of its delivery voyage the run from Nantucket Light (New York) to Tarifa in Spain. Of course, *Catalonia*, at 91 metres, was a significantly bigger ship than the 74-metre record-holder—approximately double the volume. To get the ship ready in time, Incat adopted a novel approach to delivery of the four huge Caterpillar engines from Spain: they flew them out, two per flight, in the world's biggest cargo aircraft, the Antonov An-124—by far the biggest aircraft ever to land at Hobart's modest airport. Once again, Hobart's favourite son was grabbing the local headlines.

The Hales record attempt went without incident. There was one mid-Atlantic storm to negotiate but no wave over 4 metres and, as they approached the coast of Spain, the waves actually provided a bit of help as they surfed down the faces at about 45 knots. As they burned fuel, *Catalonia* went faster; so fast in fact that they decided it was worth trying to set another record—the first ship ever to sail more than 1000 nautical miles in a day. They managed it: 1015 nautical miles at an average of 42.3 knots. An hour and a half later, at 10.30 pm local time, they arrived at their destination. *Catalonia* had covered the 2972.5 nautical miles in just 76 hours and 32 minutes—at an average speed of 38.88 knots. The Blue Riband passed from *Hoverspeed Great Britain* and Sea Containers (registered in Bermuda) to *Catalonia* and Buquebus, South America.

Within a month, the Danish and German Government-owned Scandlines took delivery of their fourth Incat vessel—the 91-metre *Cat-Link V* (hull 049). Their attack on the record aimed to set an average speed of over 40 knots (approximately 70 kilometres per hour) for the somewhat shorter crossing from New York to Bishop Rock. The Danish/German effort was much more eventful. After steaming for 12 hours at a very satisfactory average of 38.6 knots they were well up on *Catalonia*. On the second morning, the speed was up to 43 knots and the voyage average had risen to 40.28 knots. Then they got a relayed Mayday message advising all shipping to keep a sharp lookout for a ditched single-engined aircraft not far from their position. Immediately, Captain Claus Kristensen set off to the plane's last recorded position and proceeded to do a methodical search of the area. Eventually, relieved of duty by the rescue coordinators, *Cat-Link V* returned to the turnaround point to resume the crossing (no one ever found the lost aircraft).

When they resumed, the weather was not as friendly, the winds were up to 30 knots and the oncoming seas were on the beam, so they were forced to reduce engine revs to conserve the remaining fuel. They still had 770 nautical miles to go and they were averaging 40.5 knots. As they got closer to Europe, and the weather improved, they were able to pour on the speed, so much so that they crossed the Bishop Rock line doing 47.6 knots (about 90 kilometres per hour). They had certainly broken the record—all depended on the

Hales Trophy trustees' calculation of the time they had lost during the search and rescue operation at sea. Their calculations added up to a remarkable average speed of 41.284 knots—and a new record. What's more, they had managed to up the 24-hour record to 1018.5 nautical miles. So the Uruguayan businessmen's month of glory passed to Denmark and to a state-owned organisation. As it happens, Incat was in a financial partnership with the Danish and German governments at that time, but they were happy to let the Danes grab all the credit—especially as Robert Clifford was about to become the Consul-General for Denmark Down Under.

At the time of writing, *Cat-Link V* is at work for Fjord Lines under the name of *Fjord Cat*, plying the route between Kristiansand in Norway and Hanstholm in Denmark, having served in between as *Mads Mols* on the Baltic and as *Incat 049* between Trinidad and Tobago. She still holds the Atlantic record and is still entitled to fly the Blue Riband from her mast. The length of the actual pennant, by convention, is 41.284 feet in accordance with the record—41.284 knots!

PART FIVE

A test of character

The central character survives
an ordeal and emerges
unchastened

37

Clouds on the horizon

Incat entered the new millennium apparently in good shape, although the firm had not actually sold a ship for cash since 1998. Arguably, the stickiness in the world fast ferry market had set in from 1997. Incat were flattered by the fact that in 1999 they delivered no fewer than four ships to Spanish operators (at about A$70 million per unit), thus single-handedly reversing an Australian trade deficit with that country). The company had thus become a national asset in the struggle for Australia's worldwide commercial fortunes. But the contracts for sale were becoming increasingly complex as leasing firms came on the scene, and more and more value was left locked up in the vessels as they passed through various hands to final use.

The majority of ferry operators around the world don't actually own their ships—they charter or lease them from financiers. So, if Incat's production did get ahead of demand, it might have been necessary to transfer a finished ship to a holding company, perhaps Incat Chartering, or even to take back an older ferry in part-exchange to make room for the new. But that meant taking on the problem of selling-on that ferry. Sometimes, Incat even took shares in the purchasing company as part of the price. The firm's bankers were somewhat nervous about these developments and watchful of the impact on cash flow. But, at the time of writing, none of these investments has turned sour.

But the implications of all this were that, by 1999, the company's wealth was increasingly tied into long-term value all around the world rather than cash in the bank. The underlying wealth was essentially unaltered, but the firm was increasingly asset-rich and cash-poor. And still the Prince of Wales Bay boatyard was forging ahead with production. Craig Clifford's description is telling: 'The hungry beast of a production line was roaring ahead and feeding that beast was becoming a huge challenge, particularly when the bank started getting more and more nervous.'

In June 1999, Robert Clifford, aged 56, had handed over the managing directorship of the shipyard to his son Craig, then 32 years of age, and assumed the chairmanship of the company. It was a sort of 'retirement' but it was presented to the world, and to the financial press, as a shift of the company's founder to its European hub. After all, Robert Clifford remained the man who understood best the intentions and capabilities of all the main ferry operators, most of them based in Europe—and he remained the company's main super-salesman. So he shifted his main base to the unlikely setting of stockbroker-belt Surrey—the ancient town of Woking. It is indeed strategically located—25 minutes from central London and 25 minutes from Heathrow airport, and Clifford had long since learned to look on the Boeing 747 as kind of secondary office (after the Shipwright's Arms in Battery Point). His new base was within 1600 kilometres of 20 of the biggest ferry-operator customers.

For years, Incat had maintained an office in Copenhagen—so important was the Baltic Sea for the fast ferry market—and Robert Clifford had been made the Honorary Consul for Denmark in Hobart (with jurisdiction throughout Tasmania) since 1998. The Bentley Turbo R even now sports a consular number plate. Judy

Benson, whose role in the Hobart headquarters was assistant to the chairman, was appointed Vice Consul in 2002. Her car has the consular plate too. Benson came into the company from a successful career in television journalism and she became an essential prop and adviser, especially on the external relations front.

The truth is that, although Robert Clifford presents to the world as an archetypal 'man's man' or tough guy, in reality he relates much more easily to strong women, so it's not surprising that one of his key business associates should be female. That is likely an outcome of the fraught and competitive relationship with his father Fred (for whom nothing was ever good enough), and the correspondingly loving and indulgent relationship with his mother and granny (she of the full Meccano set). It was quite a tough childhood so he had to learn to be tough, but the happiest times were spent reading poetry in the quieter moments with his dad. That love of poetry persisted—under the rough exterior lies a sentimental bloke (indeed, C.J. Dennis is another hero).

Then, in 2004, to cement the Danish–Tasmanian relationship, the Danish Crown Prince married Hobart's Mary Donaldson and Robert Clifford had to be part of the Australian celebrations in Copenhagen. Incat's European and financial services head Leith Thompson had long since based himself partly in Woking and Copenhagen. So Clifford's shift to Europe and to Woking made business sense, but he continued to spend up to half his time in Australia every year and to call all the main shots in Hobart.

Clifford's UK base of Woking is also located on the Basingstoke Branch of the British canal system, connected to the Thames (and all the English canals) via the Wey Navigation to Weybridge. This is a man, we must remember, addicted to messing about on boats. Some people are amused by the idea of the creator of the world's fastest ships taking to a traditional narrow boat for recreation. Of course, Robert Clifford's narrow boat is state-of-the-art, but its maximum speed is not much more than the canal system's speed limit—4 miles per hour. If you are invited on holiday in

England with Robert Clifford, you will spend it agreeably on the water—taking orders from the skipper of the *Time Out*, working the locks and slowing your own pace at the same time. And every lock has at least one picturesque pub to hand.

38

Incat culture in the new millennium

So, with the new chairman officially located on the other side of the world, the essential test for Incat was the strength and resilience of both its business model and its sustaining corporate culture. Professor Michael Porter is not the only observer to stress the importance of culture in medium-to-big businesses, especially when the founder and prime-mover moves on (*The Competitive Advantage of Nations*, 1990). What was the nature of the beast that the young Craig Clifford was expected to mount and ride? Was it now a headless beast? By the end of the twentieth century, Incat had evolved into a subtle and complex system, arguably unique in the corporate world. In fact, the company seemed at that time to reflect the personality of its founder in three different ways: each in its own way embodying a corporate subculture. It is worth examining each in detail.

Incat as yacht

The reader will be aware by now that the art and science of yachting are somehow central to this story. Almost everybody of importance in and around the firm is a yachtsperson—and not only that, a Hobart yachtsperson, tied together with others over the years by a subtle combination of competitiveness and camaraderie. It is a bold claim that a firm of a thousand or so people could come to be treated, and to behave, as if it were a vessel—but this really was a vessel for the aspirations and creative drive of one man—and he owned the yacht (or, at any rate, more than 85 per cent of it). So Robert Clifford's characteristic approach to yacht racing was bound to become a kind of template for the conduct of Incat, particularly when it got into fierce competition with other firms. As his mother Eve Clifford said of the seven-year-old Robert Clifford: 'He had to win!'

If we accept this suggestion, a number of consequences flow. Firstly, we can predict that the Incat craft is bound to 'sail close to the wind' because this firm is dominated by its 'skipper' (rather than by its nominal board of directors). The term 'sailing close to the wind' means taking risks and going close to the limits of what is regarded as permissible or acceptable. Robert Clifford had a near-legendary reputation when it came to pushing against boundaries, and especially against any boundaries established by the 'authorities'. This was the child who largely ignored the rules and conventions at Hutchins School, virtually establishing his own private curriculum. This was the teenager who invented a whole new suite of more-or-less-within-the-rules equipment for his Derwent-class yacht to make it go faster in races. This is the adult who is happiest (on land) at the controls of a bucket excavator reclaiming land from the bay for the Incat site, and regarding the activity as 'tidying up the bay a bit!'

If you had made a prediction in the year 2000 about the likely fate of the Incat craft as it sailed into increasingly choppy commercial waters, you might well have opined: Clifford will always push it to the limits; he might even end up on the rocks (again). You would have predicted that he would never 'trim' (rein in the enterprise in the interests of prudence). So if the cautious route was to contract to build some slow ferries, thus slowing the momentum of fast ferry development, Clifford would scorn the conventional ferry route and take a chance on winning the bigger prize. Terence Daw (one-time fitout manager for Incat) has never forgotten an exchange with Robert Clifford when working on currency fluctuations for the two Ladies contract (*Pamela* and *Patricia*) back in 1985. At the time, the Australian dollar was dropping through the floor. He asked: 'Aren't you worried about this?' The reply was: 'I left school with nothing, so anything's an improvement!'

Oddly enough, the yacht racing helmsman whom Robert Clifford most closely resembles is the late Edward Heath—who won his first-ever Sydney–Hobart race (on handicap) in 1969 by stubbornly taking *Morning Cloud* miles out to sea on an eccentric route closer to the deep water winds, exactly 25 years before Robert Clifford's triumph in the same race. At that time, he was Leader of the Opposition in the United Kingdom—he would become Prime Minister the following year. He had bought *Morning Cloud*, the first yacht he had ever owned, earlier that year and immediately assembled a raucous group of super-experienced sailors to run the Sydney–Hobart challenge. It was the first British boat to win the race; an extraordinary managerial achievement.

As Prime Minister, Heath was remarkably Clifford-like: entirely without small talk, direct to the point of rudeness, opinionated to the point of stubbornness, boundlessly confident and enthusiastic, inspiring great loyalty in his followers, and inclined (as in the Sydney–Hobart race) to sail close to the wind. Heath's father had been a carpenter and his mother a lady's maid—not so far removed from Fred Clifford's butchery trade. Once he became Prime Minister his metaphorical vessel became the 'ship of state' (a Conservative administration) and he took it onto the rocks by sailing close to the wind—by picking a big fight with the trade unions (another Clifford speciality) and calling a snap election on the challenge 'who runs Britain?' He lost that fight (the 1974 election) and spent the rest of his life in a monumental sulk.

Clifford's management style was described succinctly by one of his managers in the late 1990s:

> Robert can cut to the heart of the issue very quickly. He has very little time for the superficial. He may never say 'thank you' but he will never lay people off—even to a fault. In some ways, you might say he's like the captain of a pirate ship. We're on our own out here fending for our survival, and loyalty is the glue that holds it all together. Robert is a strict taskmaster, but he'll listen to ideas that will make things run better, and his word is his bond. (Harvard Business School Case Study N9-600-149, 16 August 2000, p. 13)

If the leader of an enterprise behaves as if he is captain of some kind of vessel, it only works if all the staff buy into the metaphor. If they are mostly sailors, it's more likely that the 'skipper' notion will feel right, and take hold.

At any rate, running a biggish company (as Incat had become) as if it were a racing yacht had its perils. It was not as manoeuvrable as it used to be for one thing and decision-making could no longer be undertaken on an informed hunch. In an ocean race, what the skipper says goes: in modern business, it sometimes makes sense to listen to wise counsel, especially when the advice is to go carefully. The bigger the firm, the more important the checks and balances between the chairman and the chief executive, between all the operational executives and the independent directors—and between the 'skipper' and the extended crew.

Sometimes, however, a too-persuasive skipper can swamp all informed dissent. Incat's new competition was bigger, smarter and much more complicated. Trevor Hardstaff, the one-time Incat shipyard director, said that in the old days Robert Clifford occasionally lost a battle but always seemed to win the war by 'sheer persistence'. But once Incat got into competition with the big boys, Clifford's approach was to essay a series of tactical, guerrilla-style running battles—a bit like a tacking duel—thus running the risk that the bigger strategic war might slip away from him. The new commercial reality was getting more like protracted naval warfare than yacht racing.

Incat as feudal hamlet

Anybody walking into the Incat yard at the end of the 1990s would have been aware of another dynamic at work—that of a pre-industrial revolution manufactory; effectively a kind of small hamlet-like social system clustered around a production system and an omnipresent big boss. This, after all, was the kind of 'socio-technical' system from which Robert Clifford's great-great-grandfather William Clifford had sprung in early nineteenth century Clerkenwell. This part of London had by then become established as the seat of thousands of small workshops manufacturing watches, jewellery and associated fine craftworks. Clerkenwell and Hatton Garden remain to this day the home of gold and precious stone merchandising. That was the kind of industrial 'cluster' of interlocking and sometimes mutually supportive enterprises to which Michael Porter drew attention in his studies of national competitive advantage (ibid.).

The Prince of Wales Bay site in Hobart looks nothing like Dickensian London, but the logic of the operation is not dissimilar. There is the familiar collection of smaller firms clustered around the big 'mother ship', each serving the needs of the dominant throughput and each tied in by bonds of shared ownership and social activity. There is the same dependence on craftworking, as opposed to mass-production technology. The making of fast aluminium ships does not lend itself to mass-production because of the peculiar demands of aluminium as a material. Through the work of the co-located College of Aluminium Training, Incat had assembled a team of highly specialised welders, each working to extraordinary levels of technical finesse. To that extent, the Incat operation had become quite unlike traditional ship-building or the assembly of large aircraft on which Robert Clifford had originally based his ideas about 'sea frames' and manufacturing for stock.

As we know, the pre-industrial period of history was also dominated by feudal relations. There were plenty of emergent manufacturing operations in those times, but they existed within a social structure which usually had a feudal lord at its centre and absolute fealty as its governing principle. The morals of the lords of the various manors varied widely, but the best of them balanced the loyalty of their vassals with a compensating paternal care for all their subjects. If you offered up total loyalty, you could expect total loyalty in return. And, of course, there was no question of 'sacking' anybody—that concept had to wait for the invention of employment law. You worked for the lord unquestioningly, you brought your craft skills to the table uncomplainingly and, if need be, you might even be sent away to fight in the lord's interest. That sounds uncomfortably like the Incat company culture which grew up around its lord-and-master.

All this meant that the company's responses to the difficult market after the year 2000 were to an extent irrational, from the point of view of best business practice. A traditional board of directors would perhaps have reined in the chief executive and demanded a more prudent passage through the commercial seaways. That might have meant doing conventional things like cutting back on production in response to shrinking markets, diversifying the product mix and, above all, introducing part-time working or releasing any workers surplus to current requirements. All of these options were pressed on the 'skipper' by Craig Clifford and the other senior managers. But Incat remained essentially feudal. And Incat belonged, mostly, to Robert Clifford. So all the workers stayed on, waiting for the commercial weather to improve.

In the olden days, there was even reputed to exist a doctrine of *droit du seigneur* which, among other untrammelled powers, gave the feudal lord the right to deflower any of the local virgins in his sphere of influence. There are those who argue that Robert Clifford carries with him that same assumed right to do anything he pleases. The point is that the end-of-the-millennium Incat looked and felt a lot more like an exciting quest led by an omnipotent and heroic prince than a dull old business organisation where all the rules are written down and the professional lawyers and accountants call most of the shots. Not to mention the bankers.

Once again, an Incat manager best sums up this unusual combination of making and doing (manufacturing) with the feudal tendency:

> I think Robert wants to be the father-figure for the industry, promoting its use and developing new markets. He is relentlessly dedicated to the success of these ships. He lives and breathes these boats. He still walks into the shipyard every day [this was in 2000], watches a welder working on a bracket, and stops him and tells him a better way to assemble the part. They respect him for that. When it comes to the design, he has a vision that allows him to know what the customer needs even before they know it themselves. (ibid.)

Incat as industry 'lean' supply chain

In 1999, when Robert Clifford stepped up to the chairmanship, Incat in the technical sense was merely one ship-building company among many competing in an increasingly competitive marketplace. It would have been absurd to imagine that Incat could somehow make the market do its bidding. Yet that had long been the seductive allure of the 'lean' revolution in manufacturing pioneered by companies such as Toyota. The basic ideal was that the company would strive never to manufacture automobiles for stock because that would oblige it, through expensive marketing, to 'push' the products out the factory gate into the hands of more-or-less reluctant consumers. A key aim of the 'lean' concept was to be so market-led that all manufacturing would be 'pulled' along by carefully targeted market demand.

The streamlining of operations in Japanese manufacturing (they actually learned all this in the 1950s from the great American statistician and operations researcher W. Edwards Deming) was based on a deep and continuous understanding of, and response to, the 'demand conditions'. Never do anything unless it helps to answer the question: 'What does our existing and emergent market want and need?' In the ideal version, the company would determine your precise requirements for an automobile and then set about making you that particular, bespoke vehicle. Your order would pull your car through the system. It was never quite that simple, but that was the concept—'pull' not 'push'. The trick lay in *balancing* the push and the pull.

Robert Clifford had long since decided that organisations like Boeing provided the best business model for Incat. The big plane-makers hardly ever slackened the pace of production because the order-trail was so long. In a sense, they built 'on spec' for stock but they customised every single aircraft for the airline customer around a standard 'air frame' structure and strove for a push/pull balance. And there was a huge and stable after-market for recycled aircraft to be managed. So Incat would build standard 'sea frames' and customise each one likewise. They could standardise the manufacturing process as much as possible while allowing for variation in the input of orders—a delicate balance.

Technically, they were building boats 'on spec' so they could gain huge cost savings from standardised manufacturing procedures and usage of materials; and they would usually be in a position to supply a new vessel at short notice (sometimes ferry operators found themselves facing new market challenges suddenly). Most of Incat's competitors only started building a ship when they had an actual order in hand. Building ships continuously (four per annum), very efficiently, on spec represented Incat's USP (unique selling proposition), but it also exposed the firm to danger if the market contracted suddenly.

So the fortunes of the entire company depended in the end on Robert Clifford's continuing capacity to read the market, so that the Hobart production line could always balance the 'push' of new vessels with the 'pull' of ferry operators' intentions. If that meant reading their minds, so be it. The formula had mostly worked well in the past, probably because an ex-ferryman always has an advantage when it comes to understanding the mind-set of another ferryman. So, in a way, Incat had become more like a Japanese manufacturer than any of its direct competitors.

But the firms with which Incat was now dealing were much bigger and their decision-making was more corporate (hence slower) than inspired. Their leaders didn't on the whole seal a deal with a verbal agreement and a handshake. That was especially true of the emergent military market; the top brass rarely make up their minds quickly in peacetime, especially if there is a separate 'army' of influence-pedlars, spin-doctors and pork-barrellers stalking the lobbies of US Government.

•

So, as the new millennium unfolded, the Incat corporate character or DNA seemed to combine the tactical agility of an ocean racer, the social 'glue' of a small town or a big close-knit family, and the wit to second-guess the market. All of these facets reflected the character and personality of the founder. It would be hard to think of any 1000-person corporation which so precisely mirrored the dominant mind-set of one man. Hobart had taken its favourite swashbuckler to its heart, but nobody ever assumed smooth sailing or a rock-free passage in the future.

39

Emerging markets

Meanwhile, the Incat workforce was busy building the new bigger and improved vessels—in July 2000 rolling out the 'Evolution 10B' version of the 98-metre ship—at that time the largest ship ever built in Tasmania. She was designed specifically to cope with the notoriously rough seas of the Cook Strait crossing between New Zealand's islands. Robert Clifford, confident as ever, continued to build and invest for the long-term future, bringing a much bigger and improved construction shed on stream to make even bigger ships. He had in mind a 112-metre craft, even a 120-metre craft. And, looking even further into the future, he began a courtship with the well-established Bollinger Shipyards Inc. in Lockport, Louisiana, United States. His insight was that military all over the world needed his ships to transport matériel and men quickly to world hotspots; the alternative being to maintain ruinously expensive equipment dumps in some of the world's most inhospitable and insecure places.

As a matter of fact, it was Bollinger who sought out Incat at a fast ferry conference in 1999. They were interested in getting a slice of the US military's enormous budget for a new 'littoral combat craft' to support ground operations around the world. By then, they had taken a close look at the outstanding performance of the Incat-built HMAS *Jervis Bay* in the Timor emergency. Bollinger already had a successful track record in contracting with the US military, having built patrol boats for the Navy and every single patrol boat—more than a hundred—operated by the US Coast Guard.

Both companies understood that the infamous 'Jones Act', enacted in 1920, meant that no ship constructed outside the United States could be purchased—technically registered as a 'federally documented vessel'—by an American public body. As we know, the Americans are the great guarantors of 'free trade' all over the world, unless you happen to enter into competition with heavily-protected USA industry—and especially so in ship-building. Incat was going to need a US partner and the Bollinger family were in every way simpatico with the Cliffords—occupying a dominant place in Lockport analogous to the Incat presence in Hobart. And it was also a family company. The formal agreement to build and market high speed vessels in the United States was signed in January 2001. The joint name was to be Bollinger/Incat USA, and in August of that year the US Government awarded the new firm a charter for a multi-service program of evaluation of HSV-X1 *Joint Venture*—previously hull 050.

Robert Clifford had already leased hull 045 (previously operating on the Melbourne to Hobart run) to the Royal Australian Navy on an experimental basis—after years of persuasion. For the Navy, this really turned out to be a 'just-in-time' decision as the Timor crisis unfolded in 1999 and the renamed HMAS *Jervis Bay* earned her nickname as the 'Dili Express', transporting matériel over the Timor Sea continuously for the two years of the emergency. If Robert McKee were advising a young scriptwriter on Incat plot twists, he would likely recommend a patriotic and humanitarian role for a fast ferry in a military service setting at this point in the story—just to reinforce the military plot-twist. You couldn't make it up.

In those two years of supporting the International Force for East Timor (INTERFET) peacekeeping task force, HMAS *Jervis Bay* made 107 trips over the 430 nautical miles from Darwin to Dili, racking up over 100 000 nautical miles and carrying 20 000 passengers, 430 military vehicles and about 5600 tonnes of freight—all at high speed and with total reliability. The whole fast ship world watched her performance—from Bollinger themselves to the US Army, Navy and Marines. (In passing, hull 045's next manifestation was as *SpeedOne*, pioneering a new low-cost crossing from Dover to Boulogne. These boats can pop up anywhere.)

Contracting with the Royal Australian Navy turned out to be surprisingly simple once there was an emergency to hand. The Navy approached Incat about a fortnight before the Timor crisis exploded, taking the company into their confidence on the military intelligence and asking what ship might be available. As it happened, hull 045 was sitting in Prince of Wales Bay. The whole deal was put together in 10 days, by which time the ship had been painted grey and a very big 45 applied to the prow. When she left for Dili under Navy command, she was undoubtedly the only warship in the world equipped with two bars and a duty-free shop. The Navy's number one Mr Fix-it—Commodore Tim Cox, an unusually businesslike military man—made it all happen fast. He became a good friend and promoter of Incat. He is now, in retirement, race director of the Sydney–Hobart yacht race.

So HMAS *Jervis Bay* played a key role in alerting the US military to the potential of very fast big ships. According to Australian Navy sources, the Americans who were engaged in joint exercises in and around East Timor found themselves perplexed by a very fast-moving object on the radar screen. The commanding admiral demanded to know what craft could possibly be skirting their route at about 45 knots. It turned out to be the Australian Navy taking the opportunity to show the Americans a thing or two about nautical speed by pouring on the power in a nearly empty *Jervis Bay* on her way home to Darwin and 'buzzing' the Americans on the way. From that moment on, the admiral determined that they had to get their hands on one of these vessels—it was inappropriate for the US Navy to be shown up in this fashion!

Accordingly, the admiral, a man of action, turned up a few days later on board *Incat Tasmania*, the first of the Evolution 10B 98-metre wave-piercers, which was moored in Sydney Harbour as a trade platform for the Olympics. Within a week he negotiated for Incat's Nick Wells, supported by a draughtsman and his computer (containing all the CAD/CAM designs of the craft) to fly to Newport, Rhode Island, to the US Navy's war gaming centre. On their first afternoon, the Incat contingent fed the Navy's require-ments into the computer and came up with a reconfigured hull 050, newly arrived back from New Zealand waters, exactly tailored to US requirements. That was all it took. The only problem was for the military to find a budget appropriation to lease the vessel from Incat. That problem was 'solved' by splitting the costs between a raft of budget heads—a kind of creative accounting. So hull 050 was leased by the Army, the Navy, the Marines, the Coast Guard and the Special Operations Corps—and on a weekly basis! That made Incat's bankers nervous but it was a common trick in the US military while the various commanders scrounged around for proper long-term funding.

Robert Clifford had understood for a long time the overwhelming advantages of his kind of fast ship for the military. But once the Americans got their hands on Incat vessels—leased not sold, courtesy of the Jones Act—they began to persuade themselves. For one thing, they determined straightaway that their biggest military transport aircraft (the C-5 Galaxy) could uplift no more than two of the Army's main battle tanks, the 56–68 tonne M1 Abrams—and that over quite a short range. The US Air Force's C-17 managed to uplift one and the C-130 could not get off the ground at all with an Abrams aboard.

By contrast, the latest Incat 112-metre craft can carry 16 M1s, together with all their crews and supporting matériel, at twice the speed of any other transport ship, and unload everything in shallow water without port facilities (courtesy of a nifty onboard Incat-designed exit ramp). As Colonel Michael Toal (then Director of Combat Developments for Army Transportation) put it: 'In an unsafe world, speed is an even more priceless commodity. You can't buy back time. Once it has passed it has passed forever.' This is eerily reminiscent of Robert Clifford's insight about yacht racing: 'There is no such thing as a postponed decision [in yacht-racing] because in 10 minutes time it's a different decision!'

It is probably significant that the loudest praise comes not from navies, often hidebound by their own traditions (why do they continue to build destroyers at all?), nor from air forces (who have the luxury of doing war from a great altitude), but from the armies that in the end settle matters on the ground. Here is Major-General Robert Dail's opinion (US Army):

> I'm not hung up on catamaran design hull, but I am hung up on speed—45 knots. I am hung up on moving people with my equipment. In a battle situation, the ship can bring 40 Strykers—two companies—to a hotspot very quickly. It doesn't require a lot to load this vessel and it doesn't take a lot to unload. Incredibly, the ship requires a minimum water depth of only 15 feet in which to operate. In practical terms, that increases the number of ports accessible to the ship by a factor of five. That's an awesome thought—we establish warfare on our terms, not the enemy's! (interviewed by Christopher Holton, WorldTribune.com, 14 February 2003)

(The Stryker is the US Army's eight-wheel drive armoured combat vehicle—a sort of trackless light tank.)

It is important to remember that Robert Clifford never set out to design a 'littoral combat craft' for military applications. That is what specialist firms in the military sector do. Until Bollinger came on the scene, Clifford (the inventor) was engaged, as ever, with 'building a better mousetrap' or, as he put it, 'improving the breed' (of wave-piercing high-speed craft). Clifford is a purist, just like James Dyson, whose aesthetic sense was offended by the sheer inefficiency and wastefulness of the way that conventional vacuum-cleaners sucked air through a porous bag.

If you get the fundamental design principles right, eventually an application is likely to turn up. If you make a fast ship which offers huge versatility and a fuel-saving power-to-weight package, eventually the military is going to take notice. But for an inventor, as opposed to a proper businessman, that is a by-product of the central aesthetic quest for perfection, rather than the primary task. Robert Clifford was offended by the wastefulness of heavy steel monohulls shifting unnecessary quantities of water out of the way in order to make a passage.

40

The dramatic reverse

All this long-term strategic development of ship-building capacity and international linkages is pretty much what the textbooks would expect from an expanding firm. For more than two years, however, dating from mid-1998, Incat didn't contract to sell any ships for cash. The prospects were there and Clifford, understanding his customers' businesses as well as they did themselves, knew they had to be buying (or leasing) in due course—especially the US military.

His confidence, as usual, was undimmed but as the completed spec-built ships began to stack up in Prince of Wales Bay, it became increasingly difficult to *look* successful. There are fewer things more difficult to conceal than a 98-metre ship—or four—especially in a small and compact town like Hobart. It would perhaps have been wiser to cut back on production and staff more drastically (they reduced the workforce by some 20 per cent during that period; not quickly enough for their bankers' satisfaction) but Clifford, feeling himself to be the *paterfamilias* of all the Incat staff, plunged on. That had been his assumed and unelected role ever since the Tasmanian fishing boats followed his lead into the southern New South Wales scallop grounds in the 1970s. Loyalty is much prized in those rather old-fashioned circles. And, confident that the market would turn, he didn't fancy the bother and expense of rehiring the most skilled of his highly trained staff.

But Incat no longer had the fast ferry business to itself. Arguably, it remained the leader of the pack, but its very success in opening up a new market had inevitably attracted imitators and competitors around the world. It took some time for the emerging market to understand the dynamics of very fast ferries and, in particular, what it costs to bring a money-making (for the new owner) ferry to the market. In the process, a number of new entrant ship-builders exited ingloriously and a number of ferry operators made the painful discovery of how expensive it can be to operate an attractive-looking poorly constructed boat. The Clifford market differentiation aimed to provide progressively bigger ships with built-in advantages of passenger and crew comfort and safety, making full use of the satellite suppliers on the Prince of Wales Bay site. They called it 'improving the breed'—as if they were stock and cattle agents. And, because the design was sound, the ships burned relatively less fuel than the competition. But much of the market had yet to learn these lessons.

41

The great rival

The fiercest ship-building competitor of all turned out to be another Australian company. The Perth-based Austal Ships was only set up in 1988, just at the point when Incat was incubating the first 75-metre wave-piercer. So, as usual, Clifford and Incat showed the way. Within just seven years, Austal grew to become the world's leading manufacturer of conventional 40-metre aluminium passenger catamarans and the dominant supplier to the Asian market. And, by the late 1990s, it had become a major competitor for military sales in the United States and for State and Federal Government industrial support in Australia. Austal formed a partnership with Bender Shipbuilding of Mobile, Alabama, in the United States, at about the same time as Incat linked up with Bollinger—and for the same reason—getting round the Jones Act. In 2006, the battle turned nasty when Austal launched a long-running lawsuit against Incat, claiming that Incat had leaked a report (commissioned by Austal) which showed some of their designs in an unflattering light. At the time of writing, the Western Australians persisted with this claim.

It was however a remarkable thing, and a legitimate cause for patriotic pride, that a very substantial part of the new global market for big, fast aluminium ships should be dominated by just two companies located on the 'wrong' side of the world for the main ferry routes and operators. Australia doesn't have a particularly strong record of manufacturing except, we might argue, when the enthusiasm and cleverness of sailors is released. Austal also had the advantage that Alan Bond had started his Perth-based campaign for the America's Cup by building his yachts in aluminium alloy. Some of the Austal founders were caught up in that great adventure.

The Australian export economy has always been dominated by pastoral and extractive industries because Australia is lucky enough to have lots of valuable minerals and plenty of land for animals to graze on. So the building of high-tech fast ships represented a surprising development for the nation's economy—explicable only if you put together sailors, fishermen, aluminium and crustaceans (Austal's origins lay partly in fast boats to garner rock-lobsters; Incat's precursor company, in Clifford's fishing days, went slowly after crayfish).

Britain dominates Formula 1 racing-car construction because it happens to have a long tradition of technically savvy 'petrolhead' enthusiasts. New Zealand dominates yacht design and racing for a similar reason—a whole subculture of competitive sailing. Michael Porter might observe (in the context of culture) what a wonderful thing it is for a landlocked country like Switzerland to win the America's Cup yacht racing competition under New Zealand guidance and leadership. So together (though bitter rivals) Incat and Austal successfully took on the world.

The 'business model' that Austal adopted contrasted starkly with Clifford's and Incat's. It was much more conventional, becoming a normal public company within a few years of its founding, answerable to its shareholders and working through a board of widely experienced directors. It listed on the Australian Stock Exchange in 1998. Compared with Incat, Austal went for diversification—configuring itself to enter any ship-building market that might turn a profit. For example, in 1997, just as Incat was racing to churn out the new 91-metre fast cats, Austal bought OceanFast—a maker of boutique cruisers and luxury motor yachts—the kinds of 'gin palaces' (heavy, over-elaborated and possibly tasteless) that Robert Clifford scorned. He was, after all, a sailor—dedicated to light weight, speed and fitness-for-purpose. The obvious benefit of diversification is a buffering of the firm from trading reverses in one market or another. The downside is that you risk losing focus—as when Austal accepted the A\$70 million prestige contract to build the super yacht *Aussie Rules* for the golfer Greg Norman.

This aquatic temple to bling (complete with swimming pool, helicopter pad, theatre, etc.) was so expensive to build it lost the firm some A\$15 million. (Norman, by the way, promptly sold the monstrosity for a nice profit to Wayne Huizenga, the founder of Blockbuster Video.) *Aussie Rules* nicely symbolises the difference in the two business philosophies; Robert Clifford is, by comparison, monk-like in his dedication to the perfect wave-piercer as the correct, ordained solution to the size versus weight versus speed equation. *Aussie Rules* was made mainly of aluminium but it was very heavy and, you might argue, pointless. When Incat got into financial bother, Clifford absolutely refused to take orders to build a couple of tugboats. But he never was an ordinary businessman, subject to the prevailing wisdom of the business school. He had always been an inventor with a need for a creative outlet. That outlet happened to be his own (mostly) A\$200 million business.

Austal meanwhile continued to expand by acquisition, in 1998 purchasing Image Marine, a well-established maker of fishing and patrol boats. Within a short time, Austal was building fast boats for the Australian Customs fleet, patrol boats for the New South Wales Water Police, the Navy and the Yemeni Government, and also specialised 'live aboard' vessels for adventure tourism and diving. And, ominously, Austal bought an aluminium shipyard in Tasmania (in business they call this 'parking your tanks on somebody else's lawn') and launched a marketing assault on the US military. Austal picked up its first 'theatre support vessel' order in 2001—the same year as Incat's breakthrough into the US military market, and it continued to win lucrative new American orders.

42

Ill omens

Quite apart from the drought in sales, for the superstitiously minded, there were other adverse omens for Incat. At the very end of the twentieth century, Robert Clifford, as the owner of more than 85 per cent of Incat's equity, had entered the Australian *Business Review Weekly*'s list of Australia's 200 richest men. The unions at Incat duly took note. In May 2000, Incat suffered its first serious stoush over the pay of the shipyard workers. The Australian Manufacturing Workers Union demanded a 5 per cent pay rise and a 38-hour week, based on their discovery that the company had made a A$53 million paper profit the year before. With Robert Clifford safely ensconced in Woking, it was left to the new managing director (Craig Clifford) to explain the realities of accounting practice to the workers. The firm had indeed made a 'profit', but it remained very asset-rich and very cash-poor (until they succeeded in selling another ship for cash).

So it didn't help matters that the personal fiefdom of one of Australia's richest men was seen to be so profitable. The great Sir John Harvey-Jones of ICI fame always said that the moment a firm started to line the headquarters' atrium with marble (that is, to flaunt its wealth) was the moment to sell its stock (*Getting It Together*, 1991). The Greek term *hubris* ('insolence, overconfidence, such as invites disaster or ruin') is meant to describe that kind of ostentation. And then, to cap it all, Incat gloried in a ceremonial visit from the Queen and Duke of Edinburgh in March 2000. The Queen and Eve Clifford had a nice chat about recalcitrant sons. As if that weren't enough ceremonial, the 98-metre *Incat Tasmania*, launched in July, carried the Olympic flame for part of its journey from Kingston to Port Arthur and ended up parked in Sydney Harbour as a floating conference venue for the Australian Trade Commission. All this meant that Incat had arrived triumphantly on the public relations front, but the real-world market for big fast catamarans stubbornly refused to budge. Still no sales.

Worse was to come. In the course of 2001, the Australian Navy decided not to renew the lease for HMAS *Jervis Bay*. She had done her job magnificently during the Timor emergency, but the Navy couldn't think of a role (or a budget head) for her into the future, even though she had single-handedly become the public face of the Australian military in times of civilian crisis. This was just at the time that the US military was beginning to experiment seriously with the notion of the 'littoral combat craft'—for which a fast lightweight ferry seemed to be perfectly suited. On top of that, the Tasmanian Government decided against buying a new and bigger Incat ferry for the Bass Strait run, settling instead for a couple of big monohulls from Europe. Truth to tell, they had had some problems with the serviceability of the 96-metre *Devil Cat* (hull 050) in rough weather. But insiders suggest that the real reason for the decision to go for conventional ships lay in the trade unions' influence over the state's Labor Government.

In a way, the new bigger Incat ships were victims of their own technical superiority, because their speed allowed them to operate with just 35 shore-based crew. The alternative, much more attractive to the maritime unions, was two crews of about 120 per ship living on board, alternating with a month's holiday entitlement. Deployment of Incat craft would have meant huge savings of taxpayers' money but the loss of about 200 jobs—the price of progress. Meanwhile, shipyard production had actually been slowing since the beginning of 2000 and the consequent withdrawal of overtime working had been one trigger for the 24-hour strike in May of that year. Arguably, the strength of the maritime unions had exported a problem to Incat's engineering unions. Everything is connected. By July 2001, the workforce was down to 750, from a peak of just over 1000 in 1996.

And there were other portents; on the evening of 11 September 2001, the first US military chartered vessel (hull 050, the ex-*Devil Cat*) left the Hobart wharf for the long voyage to the United States. All the Incat staff who had been farewelling their new friends and comrades got home to the twin towers news on the television. *Joint Venture* was sailing back to a different and more dangerous situation, but she would turn out to be exactly the right boat for that new world. The shock of the terrorist attack paralysed business decision-making for a period, maybe especially in the US military, although in the longer run it probably helped Incat's ambition to sell them quick-response solutions.

Finally, on 5 November 2001, Robert's father Fred died. He had never been the same since the trotter kicked him in the chest 11 years before, so his death was sad rather than tragic—but it looked like one more omen in Incat's oncoming *annus horribilis*. All that was needed now for dramatic effect was a bankruptcy or something like it. But Incat's bankers were, it seemed, unlikely to make life difficult. After all, every airport in Australia sported National Australia Bank advertisements boasting of its key partnership role in providing long-term support for the development of Incat's worldwide business.

43

A short history of a receivership

Incat's great drama of 2002 was essentially a titanic struggle of Robert Clifford, now officially resident in Woking, against the bankers—of National Australia Bank (NAB) in particular (the firm's bankers) but also against the banking 'profession'. On 21 March 2002, and after many months of negotiation and last-ditch marketing effort, NAB wrote to Incat to ask for its A$75 million back by the end of the week. That is how a receivership is generally launched. This particular receivership lasted 11 months and it cost Incat, conservatively, A$20 million and, of course, severely dented its worldwide reputation. Whether it harmed Robert Clifford's image in Hobart is a separate question as it had been some time since he had monopolised the headlines. The bank was absolutely within its rights to launch the action, but it certainly displayed a failure of trust—born of mutual incomprehension and some bad faith.

Since then, the banking profession's reputation has taken a knock. In 2009, at the time of writing, few people take the pretensions of bankers to accountability or competence very seriously. Indeed, taxpayers all over the world are being obliged by their governments to bail out the bankers from a disaster of their own making. Many detect that self-reinforcing combination of arrogance and stupidity to which the great psychoanalyst Wilfred Bion drew attention— arrogance makes you stupid and stupidity leads to arrogance ('On Arrogance', *International Journal of Psychoanalysis*, vol. 39, 1958, pp. 144–6). Worse still, the only people that governments around the world can think of to sort out the mess are more bankers.

Due to the drought of sales, Incat owed the NAB A$75 million and, from early 2002, the State of Tasmania another fully-secured A$30 million. There was nothing unusual in this state of affairs as they had owed substantially more in the past and Incat's various assets in Tasmania and around the world covered the exposure comfortably, and that didn't include the completed ships which were in play for various potential buyers—one of which was sold just a month after the administrator stepped in, clearing more than half the debt at a stroke. One of the peculiarities of receivership accounting is that a magnificent A$70 million fast ship is not treated as an 'asset'. Another peculiarity is that, if the bank should destroy your reputation by foreclosing prematurely on your debts, you would be unwise to sue for defamation because the bank's pockets will always be deeper than yours.

Until the breakdown of trust, Craig and Robert Clifford and their colleagues had had a healthy relationship with their principal 'relationship' banker inside NAB. Most of the big banks, indeed most big businesses, now pretend that business deals are actually 'relationships'—it seems friendlier and more civilised somehow. At any rate, NAB's 'relationship' man at Incat had come to understand the peculiarities of the fast ferry business quite well by then. Suddenly, the bank replaced him and within a week his replacement fell ill with a nervous breakdown. The bank seems to have been under a certain amount of strain at that time. His subsequent replacement, in turn, lasted just a few months and proved unable to cope with the complexity of the case. He was, after all, being asked to encompass the complex demands of a completely unfamiliar type of business. Judgements about solvency are largely technical, but judgements about the sustainability and resilience of a firm call for a higher level of judgement—and that calls for a higher level of understanding and intellectual grasp on the part of human beings—not upon formulae.

It was at that point that the bank's overall head of 'credit restructuring' Ray Pridmore was obliged, because all the relationship bankers had fallen by the wayside, to take on the Incat case-load just at the point when he was also personally burdened with both the Ansett and the HIH Insurance insolvencies—two of the biggest and most controversial business catastrophes in Australian history. More worrying still, he was dealing simultaneously with very similar difficulties in Incat's arch-rival Austal. They were subject to exactly the same market stickiness as Incat. Reportedly, Pridmore had already been alarmed by a cover of *Incat the Magazine* in early 2001—'4 SHIPS 4 SALE'—a novel approach to marketing ships, redolent of the automobile sales forecourt. That was typical of Clifford's chirpy optimism; his colleagues in the firm were less persuaded of the wisdom of this approach. It was all a bit too unconventional for Ray Pridmore.

So there was a failure of continuity and, it seems, of focus. Clifford, perhaps too trustingly, believed he had a continuing understanding with the NAB, based on verbal assurances and historical good faith. That was how he had always done business in the past. Pridmore certainly worked long and hard to try to avert the administration. In the fast ship business, a handshake and a verbal commitment is generally enough. Robert Clifford's memory of his last one-to-one meeting with Pridmore are of the reassurance: 'If you have a problem, call me—at any time.' Then, ominously, his phone calls weren't answered.

There is no way of knowing for sure what transpired at that last fateful meeting between Robert Clifford and Ray Pridmore. The odds are that the two men emerged from the meeting with quite different views on what took place. Afterwards, Clifford told his family and associates that it had 'gone well!' But ever since the swimming meet back in 1958 (the one where he won everything, broke all the records and told his mum he did 'not too bad'), Robert Clifford had been offering monosyllabic and taciturn accounts of reality. He had always been both optimistic to a fault and cryptic in delivery. Mostly, the Incat senior management liked to send along a sidekick to important meetings—just to check what really happened. Like most gifted people, Robert Clifford tends to overwhelm meetings with his confidence and optimism and, sometimes, misses the underlying point—particularly if the news is bad. So, despite all the months of uncertainty, the receivership still came as a bombshell to the man himself.

As we now know, NAB was itself sailing into trouble at that time with the collapse of its disastrous US investment in the HomeSide Lending business (a A$3.6 billion write-off). Within another two years, a failure of the bank's compliance regime permitted the incubation of a nest of rogue foreign currency traders within the bank that cost a further A$360 million. And there was another A$409 million write-off following a failed 'integrated systems implementation' software investment. All of these blunders by the bank can be seen as forerunners of the general banking collapse of 2008—and NAB turned out to be as exposed to the chimera of derivatives trading as any other major bank in that general collapse. Perhaps it was just bad luck for Incat to be exposed to the vagaries of this particular bank at that particular time. As it happens, over the whole period Incat never even exceeded the bank's credit facility.

It was all a far cry from the estimable Tony Travers, manager of the Sandy Bay branch of the ANZ Bank, who made the initial investment of A$10 000 in the Sullivan's Cove Ferry Company (Incat's precursor) in 1972. Travers was an old-fashioned banker—a local manager with a good understanding of the local economy and of the Cliffords' and their partners' track records. But that was in the days when the clearing banks simply lent and borrowed money and kept a small percentage for themselves at the margins.

Investment and merchant banking were quarantined from that homely activity.

It seems that in 30 short years, the banking 'profession' morphed from Tony Travers to Gordon 'greed is good' Gekko (the anti-hero of Oliver Stone's movie *Wall Street*); from informed investment to detached money-making and to the introduction of systems and formulae incomprehensible to ordinary people—even to most bankers. In 2002, NAB, in need of money, having taken a gloomy view of the situation and no longer really understanding the Incat business, simply wanted its money out first (and certainly before the Tasmanian Government got its money back). Through the receivership, NAB achieved 'first priority lender' status.

So Incat's genuine predicament—no sales for nearly two years—was compounded by a bank in some kind of panic. As if coping with HIH, Ansett, Austal and Incat simultaneously wasn't enough, NAB's extraordinary losses quickly brought it under pressure to cut costs, and so to call in the last resort—McKinsey & Company (the US management consultants) to advise on 'restructuring' the bank. In the financial world, McKinsey are acknowledged as the 'go-to' consultants for cost-cutting. That meant, predictably, sacking 3400 staff and closing down 56 branches (of the kind that Tony Travers used to run so usefully for another bank). McKinsey's unsurprising advice to NAB was to focus attention on the bank's services in support of 'wealth management', that is, making the rich richer, not serving the interests of ordinary people and small to medium-sized Tasmanian businesses. Ironically, Tony Travers' old bank (the ANZ) offered to buy all the closed branches but NAB, still playing hard ball, turned them down. All this was going on in parallel with Incat's financial difficulty.

44

Bankers in general

There is bound to be a philosophical gulf between the quint-essential man of action and reality (Clifford) and a raft of people (bankers) who have elected to spend their professional lives in the symbolic world—in the world of money. Throughout his life, Clifford never embarked on any venture without constructing a meticulous physical model first. Balsawood carvings of ships and racing cars morphed into scientific ocean trials and tank testing, but the aim was always to find out what would happen in the real world of physics. The small model of the first wave-piercing craft was lovingly crafted from Huon pine, such was its perceived importance. By the end of the twentieth century, most big businesses were operating according to one 'business model' or another, and most of those models were invented by the big management consultants. And, more to the point, all the big international banks were, lemming-like, operating according to exactly the same business model as each other. It turned out to have no connection with reality whatsoever. The word 'model' along with 'relationship' and a host of other previously meaningful words had been mangled by big business.

History has never looked kindly on the usurers—and many religions have cast them out. (Jesus Christ, we should never forget, took an exceedingly dim view of the financial services industry.) Dante, in *The Divine Comedy*, placed the usurers in the inner ring of the seventh circle of Hell—below even the suicides. The usurers' ring was shared by the blasphemers and the sodomites. So much for bankers. Once money became the main lubricant for human economic affairs and modern banks emerged in the sixteenth century, we have needed men and women of good intelligence and good faith to regulate its flows. In his annual (2003) letter to investors, the 'Sage of Omaha' (Warren Buffett) described the bankers' derivative products as 'financial weapons of mass destruction', precisely because they had no real substance. Buffett always took the view that any product that couldn't be explained to your granny was probably without substance.

So the travails of Incat in 2002 symbolised mutual incomprehension. To be fair, there are still bankers around the world whom we can admire. Tony Travers, now in retirement in Queensland, is obviously one; and the most famous of all is Mohammad Yunus—the pioneer of microfinance. He had the bright idea of lending money not to rich men in search of more wealth, but to poor women in search of security, enterprise and community renewal—to real people. Thus the Grameen Bank in Bangladesh reinvented banking, just as Robert Clifford reinvented fast sea travel. If you build a better mousetrap . . .

In practice, the NAB—via their agents the administrators (David McEvoy of the accountants PricewaterhouseCoopers)—proceeded against only three of the nine Incat companies: Incat Tasmania (which built the ships), Incat Australia (which sold them) and Incat Chartering. These were the companies where they thought any spare money might be lurking. Jeff Kelly, the very experienced head of the Tasmanian Department of State Development (who had a hand in the government's loan of A$30 million to Incat in 2001) laughed when he learned of the bank's action, and not just because he regarded it as misconceived but also because he predicted, accurately, that the receivers would never be able to get their heads around the international complexity of Incat's affairs. To start with, the 14 ships in which Incat had a greater or lesser stake were dotted all around the world and their 'value' was almost impossible to assess. And realising that value was something else again.

If you force a fire sale, you run the risk of destabilising the entire world fast ferry market by flooding it with undervalued ships. One South American company had already run into trouble and had released two Incat ships into the almost-saturated European market. As Robert Clifford later acknowledged: 'We made two ships too many!'—so delicately balanced is the world's fast ship supply chain. At the time of the receivership in 2002, there were four craft in Prince of Wales Bay or under construction. Hull 058 was completed and waiting for a buyer. Hull 059 was almost finished and hull 060 well advanced. And work had started on hull 061. Clifford, adopting the 'glass-half-full' position simply wanted to get on with making and selling the ships—absolutely confident that the target clients would make their move soon. The bank, adopting the 'glass-half-empty' position, wanted all construction and marketing activity to cease forthwith, along with all the creative design work associated with it.

Receivership is a murky business, not well-understood outside the panelled halls of the big banks and accountancy firms (and sometimes not even there). As in the old Victorian melodramas, everything is undertaken by arm's-length agents of the 'respectable' bankers. So in the Victorian version, when the bailiffs turn up, they tend to be big, scruffy fellows with a menacing mien. NAB's chief enforcer in the Incat case turned out to be a satisfyingly huge ex-murder squad detective from Scotland Yard. From the start there were low levels of trust between the parties (it did not help matters that Incat's much-respected chief financial officer had been poached by Hydro Tasmania a few months before). But part of the underlying difficulty seems to have been the receivers' frustration with the subtlety and complexity of the business itself. It was easy for them to imagine that Incat was playing games with offshore monies.

45

Politics

As it happens, Jeff Kelly, who helped to broker the Tasmanian Government loan of A$30 million late in 2001, was also a member of the delegation to the Federal Government in February of 2002, desperately seeking a temporary stay of execution for Incat. It could not have been a more high-powered meeting. Among those present were the conservative Prime Minister John Howard, the CEO of NAB Frank Cicutto (soon to be sacked with a A$3.27 million payoff), the Labor Party Premier of Tasmania Jim Bacon, the NAB 'bad bank' boss Ray Pridmore and (representing Incat) Craig Clifford and John Harris. Also present was an array of Tasmanian interested parties—from a trade union representative to the Mayor of Glenorchy. The Tasmanians thought to take along Denis Rogers, who doubled as Chairman of the State Development Board and the Australian Cricket Board. He duly talked cricket with the Prime Minister before the meeting got under way.

Ray Pridmore, on behalf of NAB, had already arrived at an agreement with Austal, the West Australian fast ferry builders, to assure its funding into the future. That agreement included a provision that Austal had to seek permission from the bank before starting to build any vessel (not the kind of restriction that Robert Clifford would ever countenance). Austal, wisely, had decided to kowtow to the bank's financial orthodoxy. Pridmore was already meeting privately with the Tasmanian Government (that is, without Robert Clifford's knowledge) to advise on the viability of Incat's recovery plans. This placed him in an awkward, perhaps even compromised, position. As adviser also to Austal, it must have been difficult for him not to form a view on which of the two competing Australian shipbuilders was likely to garner the lion's share of the upcoming US military orders. He was certainly more comfortable with Austal's conventional corporate structure and practices. It is clear from the correspondence the bank was acutely aware that in the Incat case they were dealing with the wealth of one man rather than with a 'proper' business, and he was still calling all the shots, albeit as 'chairman' and from Woking.

At the Sydney meeting, the Prime Minister is said to have listened politely to the Incat case and to have been well-enough briefed. He surprised the Tasmanian contingent by making one or two scathing remarks about banks and bankers. He also promised personally to telephone the Tasmanian Premier with the Commonwealth's decision on the Incat rescue after the following Monday's Cabinet meeting. That call never came. Instead, the Tasmanian Government actually learned the outcome from the media—from a remark by the Minister for Industry, Tourism and Resources, Ian MacFarlane. It fell to him, eventually, to make the call to advise the Tasmanian Government that there would be no Federal support for Incat. MacFarlane's horse-trading argument was that the firm had already had a recent perk from Canberra in the form of an extension of the ship-building industry's 'bounty' protection from import penetration. This was a long-running story, based on Incat organising the Australian fast aluminium ship-builders to lobby the Federal Government to delay reductions to the 'bounty' in order to protect local ship-building (against predatory pricing by heavily subsidised European ship-builders) and to protect local jobs. And by deciding not to buy an Incat ship for the Bass Strait, the Tasmanian Premier Jim Bacon made it easy for the Prime Minister to claim the Tasmanian bid for a federal bailout wasn't 'fair dinkum'. Politics again.

Ian MacFarlane's idea that Tasmania had already had its perk seems reminiscent of George W. Bush's bemusement at Dick Cheney's determination to direct even more money to the richest Americans: 'Didn't we already give them something?' (Suskind, *The Price of Loyalty*, 2004). There is a time for horse-trading and a time for decisions on principle. Meanwhile, international car-makers like Mitsubishi in South Australia were attracting huge Federal Government subsidies for 'sunset' industries in a desperate but doomed attempt to keep manufacturing jobs in Australia. And, of course, competitors like Austal were quite rightly lobbying hard in Canberra for 'fairness' to their own special interests. We can only speculate whether or not the presence of a notably left-wing State Government in Hobart harmed Incat's chances of a sympathetic hearing from a very conservative Federal Government in Canberra. That is the federal system at work.

There was another much more explosive meeting shortly afterwards between the Prime Minister John Howard, the Tasmanian Premier Jim Bacon and the CEO of NAB Frank Cicutto, supported by their advisers. At this meeting it became clear to the Tasmanians present that, if and when NAB decided to pull the plug on Incat by instituting a receivership (a contingency about which the bank had promised to give plenty of warning), then the $30 million loaned to Incat by the State Government would disappear immediately into the bank's coffers. Until that moment the State Government had assumed, perhaps naively, that in the event of receivership they would join the queue for funds with other creditors. The late Jim Bacon was well known as a gentleman—a man of dignity and self-composure. His aides had never seen him so angry.

When the administration axe falls, it falls in the form of a formal letter from the bank requesting the return of A$75 million by Friday.

Then the administrators descend, taking over the main office and occupying key seats, sacking the staff regarded as marginal to the main purpose, and winding up the business and extracting all the money. It is an unpleasant business for a respectable firm acting in good faith. Something like 95 per cent of receiverships end in bankruptcy so the enforcers are programmed to expect evasion, trickery and lots of buried financial bad news.

When the administrators arrived, Kim Clifford, by this time the Incat Director of Marketing, was overseas with a rather important client (the US military); she was actually on board *Joint Venture* (hull 050) at sea, so it took a couple of days for news of the receivership to reach her. Kim got back to Hobart to find her office locked (the receiver sacked her along with other key executives) and a demand to hand in her car keys (which would have meant getting a cab to pick up the kids from school that day). It wasn't long before the administration team were wandering down the road from the Shipwright's Arms to Robert Clifford's Hobart home in order to appraise the value of the paintings on the walls there. Those paintings, naturally, are mostly maritime scenes and the best of them, by the celebrated artist Haughton Forrest (brought up on the Solent but living mainly on the Derwent), are outstanding and, of course, pricey.

Robert Clifford was also in the United States negotiating, ultimately successfully, the lease of another ship to the military. Meanwhile, back in Hobart, Incat staff, adapted to Clifford's and Incat's customary parsimony, were somewhat unimpressed by the gung-ho young PricewaterhouseCoopers (PwC) team living in Hobart's most expensive hotels and refusing even to share a taxi to the shipyard. Absolute power never made anybody look attractive. And of course a company that quickly trades its way out of trouble, as Incat did, automatically calls into question the wisdom and competence of the bankers who precipitated the receivership in the first place. Only bankruptcy can prove them right. Meanwhile, the receivers are only doing their job.

There are too many worrying stories of big banks, in league with big accountants, bullying small firms into receivership and bankruptcy—and getting financial reward for doing so. The new business model for servicing SMEs (small to medium-sized enterprises) sometimes requires lower level bank managers to persuade small firm proprietors to adopt complex funding mechanisms which serve both to enhance bank profits and to weaken the proprietors' control over their own financial destiny. The new model certainly 'incentivises' local bank managers to sell new business, as opposed to just looking after existing clients. And sometimes local managers can, for example, enhance their own bonuses by exaggerating local property values. Most SME proprietors are not sophisticated people so they are inclined to trust the judgement and the good intentions of the 'bank manager'. They have an idealised Tony Travers in mind, rather than the typical modern young careerist bent on boosting his branch's income this year and his reputation in the bank. When banks foreclose, some of these SME proprietors sue the bank concerned. Even if they win, it costs them. As the long-retired Tony Travers now recalls, he was one of the last of the 'stand-alone' bank managers.

46

The 'Trollope Ploy'

Incat's creative response to the crisis was absolutely typical of Robert Clifford's combination of optimism, determination and ingenuity. Essentially, they behaved as if it wasn't happening at all. This is exactly the kind of eccentric response that the story-guru Robert McKee would wish to see. Unconsciously, the Incat top brass were replaying the events of another crisis—the Cuban missile stand-off of 1962—with the Clifford family replaying Robert Kennedy's inspired 'Trollope Ploy'.

On that occasion and at the height of the crisis, the Americans had received two parcels of signals from Krushchev in Moscow: one, surprisingly emollient, on a Friday; and a further much more belligerent parcel on the Saturday. They had already semi-officially sounded out the Russians on a possible formula for resolving the crisis—linking the Russians' removal of the missiles to an American promise to stay out of Cuba. The Saturday signals from the Kremlin added in the complication of dismantling American missiles in Turkey.

Roger Hilsman describes what happened next:

It was Robert Kennedy who conceived a brilliant diplomatic manoeuvre—later dubbed the 'Trollope Ploy', after the recurrent scene in Anthony Trollope's novels in which the girl interprets a squeeze of the hand as a proposal of marriage. His suggestion was to deal only with Friday's package of signals—Krushchev's cable and the approach through Scali—as if the conflicting message on Saturday, linking the missiles in Cuba with those in Turkey, simply did not exist. That message, in fact, had already been rejected in a public announcement. The thing to do now was to answer the Friday package of approaches and make the answer public—which would add a certain political pressure as well as increase the speed. (*To Move a Nation*, 1967)

As a relieved world learned over the next few days—it worked.

In the Incat case, the gloom and pessimism of NAB and PwC represented metaphorically the hawkish Saturday signals. The Incat team simply reverted to Friday—assuming that everything would be for the best in the best of all possible worlds and, crucially, going public (just like Robert Kennedy) in the eyes of the customer base around the world. Those customers had to be persuaded that the receivership was a temporary irritant and that all their long-term plans for bigger and better ships would be realised in due course. And the existing customers needed reassurance that their servicing, parts and warranty requirements would be met into the future. Without that reassurance, no customer or prospect could be expected to trade with Incat. As in aviation, the after-market had become a significant part of the business.

Incat the Magazine, for example, infuriated the receivers because it played the Trollope Ploy to the hilt—discussing exciting technical developments and future prospects with a sunny assurance—just as the receivers were trying to put a stop to all developmental and marketing activity, and to publication of the magazine itself. Continued publication was achieved by simply switching publisher to Incat's European arm, which was not subject to the receiver's order.

The editorial work continued in the editor Kim Clifford's home. The first Incat Europe magazine, which came out shortly after the administration began, even contained pages of 'for sale' craft, after the fashion of the motoring pages at the back of newspapers. This was accompanied by a very aggressive program of electronic marketing.

The chairman penned his usual column at the beginning of the magazine, under the title: 'On the Rocks'. He kicked off with a recollection of the 1994 grounding of *Condor 11* and the prophets who predicted doom for Incat then:

> The lack of confidence in the fast vessel market shown by our bankers on 21st March in calling in the receiver has once again got our detractors and competitor [presumably Austal] jumping for joy. They do so however from a position of ignorance—ignorance of our asset base and ignorance of our resolve. Shipbuilding has never been a trade for the fainthearted—just look at the long list of failed shipbuilders who are no longer trading. Little wonder why financiers show little confidence in shipbuilders. Little wonder why they finance ships only on confirmed order. Come to think of it, many builders have failed even where the orders have been in place and the money paid up front. The bottom line; we will not fail. If you have any doubt, watch this space. (*Incat the Magazine*, vol. 3, no. 16, 2002, p. 6)

Over the years, *Incat the Magazine*, a thrice-annual glossy, had won most of the trade magazine awards. Its production values were exceptionally high and its editorial content broad and engaging for any reader in or around the fast ferry business. Above all, it always focused on the ships in use, taking the point of view and business interests of the customers as its base. They say in the marketing trade that the trick lies in inhabiting the customer's mind-set. This is what Robert Clifford, ex-ferryman, had always done well, so the magazine became a regular reminder to the trade that Incat understood its customers' needs and ambitions.

What made the magazine especially unusual was its exposure in every issue of state-of-the-art technical developments, thus treating the lay reader as an earnest PhD student or high-powered professor in a technical university—all accompanied by beautifully illustrated technical drawings and photography. This was the kind of material which many firms would treat as 'commercial-in-confidence'. For Incat, unhindered by paranoia over patent, copyright and intellectual property, it represented the kind of informed, behind-the-scenes discussion you might expect to find at any trade conference. So the magazine was more than just a trade paper—it had become a reminder, three times every year, that Incat the company had become the fount of most technical exchange about the place of the fast ferry in world trade. If, as the receivers wanted, it disappeared overnight, it would send a shock through that world from which Incat might not recover. So it was the Trollope Ploy.

But, in that first off-piste edition, Robert Clifford could not restrain himself from submitting to the editor (she could hardly turn it down) a little reflection on bankers he had known throughout his career. It was entitled 'From Little Piggy to Big Piggy & the Piggies in the Middle'.

47

'Time to change banks!'

In that issue, he gave a rueful account of all his dealings, until then, with bankers. Beginning with the Hobart Savings Bank as a 10-year-old—cashed in at the end of school with earnings wiped out by inflation—Robert Clifford then managed to steer clear of banks completely until he was deep into the fishing business with the Bank of New South Wales:

> I mentioned to Dad that the proceeds of selling the old boats would go a long way to pay for a new boat. He then explained to me the error of my thinking; the funds did not even clear the overdraft! The new boat, which was very successful, was built entirely on bank overdraft funds. Tiring of the fishing business, I wanted to sell up and enter the river ferry business. The Bank said no; they would not fund a fisherman into a new ferry business. Time to change banks! (*Incat the Magazine*, vol. 3, no. 16, 2002 pp. 10–11)

Next up was the ANZ Bank and the estimable Tony Travers—a man of judgement and vision. But, not for the last time, a relationship of continuity and mutual understanding with a capable branch

205

manager was interrupted by the bank itself. When the account got too big for the local branch (the Sullivan's Cove Ferry Company had grown too successful), it was transferred from Sandy Bay to Hobart Head Office, then to Melbourne and to a succession of bank managers looking down their noses at a small Tasmanian ship-builder. *Time to change banks!* The Commonwealth Bank then solicited the account and ran it well until another enlightened manager got promoted elsewhere, to be succeeded by a series of poor-quality appointments. *Time to change banks!*

The next, and fateful, bank was the National Australia Bank and the relationship worked well until, once again, the bankers' musical chairs put paid to a business relationship based on understanding and trust. Obviously time to change banks again but—to whom? After the receivership, Incat's reputation was trammelled and the costs of banking became almost prohibitive. (At the time of writing, Incat has funded all its operations from reserves. The business model has migrated from 'Time to change banks!' to 'Never again!'). You could say that the chairman's reflections on bankers and banking in the 2002 magazine did not represent the best way of sucking up to NAB or with their agents at PwC.

More serious was the receiver's decision to close down the 30-strong design office, already ring-fenced as 'Revolution Design'. Closing off the design function, to a ship-builder, is the equivalent of mortgaging the future. The designers were the intellectual heart of the business; they could not be dispersed. They had been recruited, trained and developed over many years. So Robert Clifford immediately took them over as his personal fiefdom—a luxury only available to the majority-owner of a private company. Sometimes businesses need to move fast, as in a tacking duel. Within days, the design team was making money from outside clients as an independent outfit. Clifford, as ever, had his eye on the future. All the bankers could see was bad news in the present. Revolution Design remains a separate company to this day, but umbilically linked to the Incat parent.

48

Release

In the end, the receivership was extinguished in the only way possible—by the sale or lease of all the ships in play—just as Robert Clifford had predicted. The firm actually sold or leased four ships during the emergency. The order for hull 059 from Bay Ferries of Canada came through just a month after the receivership began. The receivers, fantasising that they had become, overnight, fast ferry marketers rather than accountants, did their best to claim credit for the sale. Robert Clifford, unsurprisingly grumpy, took the view that all they had achieved was a fire-sale price for a ship the customer already wanted and needed. He knew what the true price was. It was the Incat marketing team that pulled it off. At any rate, the sale extinguished most of the debt at a stroke. From then on, David McEvoy (the PwC administrator) began to understand that this was one receivership which was unlikely to end in bankruptcy. In fairness, he had said so from the start. The receivers did at least manage to sell a few cars.

The lease of the three ships to the US military took a little longer and required some assistance from Incat's friends and partners around the world. Incat's American ally Bollinger Shipyards invested in hull 060 (*Spearhead*) and another US investor took on hull 061 (later HSV-2 *Swift*) for onward lease to the US Navy. Bollinger, as a separate company, were legally shielded from the Incat administration and so not threatened in any way, but they were friends in need. Incat had a ship it needed to sell to get the creditors off its back, but the US military was only interested in a lease. So Bollinger chartered the vessel with money supplied by a completely independent leasing company. As Vice President of Bollinger, Chris Bollinger, explains: 'Our intent was never to buy the ships—we are not in the ship owning business, we are in the shipbuilding business. But there was a situation, as I think everybody is aware . . . at Incat and they were looking for a buyer' (interviewed by Matthew Stanley on *Stateline Tasmania*, 14 February 2003). And that is how a 98-metre fast ship, not regarded as an 'asset' at all by the administrators, turned out to have a value of A\$70 million.

In the meantime, Incat's workforce dwindled throughout 2002 from about 700 workers in March to 250 at the end of August. At the time of the receivership, Robert Clifford admitted: 'I kept on too many people for too long when we didn't have orders locked up. We should have been winding down. If I'd been tough enough we could have been down to 200–300 people today. But some of these people have been with me for 25 years and I know their wives and children.' Thus did the paternal and soft-hearted feudal lord finally confront the hard-headed businessman.

In April, he had again been sounding off about 'donkeys' in the workforce: 'Donkeys with not enough brains to make their heads ache . . . as "intelligent leaders" in tough economic times, Incat has no choice but to "cull the donkey population" for the good of the majority, and in doing so getting rid of "the weakest links".'

By August, Clifford was sentimental about the gradually dispersing Incat family. If you understand the rumbustious relationship between Robert Clifford and his father, you understand there is no inconsistency here; just because you verbally abuse some people it doesn't mean they are not family. In truth, the receivership forced

Robert Clifford's hand; until business picked up, there simply wasn't enough work for the workforce to do.

By the end of 2002, Robert Clifford's judgement about the true state of the market began to be affirmed. Hull 045 (the ex-*Jervis Bay*) went off to an Italian ferry company and hull 060 deployed to the Middle East as the US Army's TSV-1X. On 24 October, the US Navy bought hull 061 in a deal worth about A$95 million. That meant a rush of activity and re-employment in the boatyard, installing a helicopter deck and a stern ramp for loading and unloading military vehicles, including tanks and amphibious assault vehicles. Hull 059, meanwhile, was off to Bay Ferries of Canada for the Trinidad to Tobago run. And all the while hull 050 continued its service as a US joint-services trial vessel, deployed to various trouble spots around the world.

Since then, these ships have had a busy and versatile life in their 'military' role. For example, *Swift*, the Navy's HSV (high speed vessel) played a key part in two disaster relief operations—Operation Unified Assistance for survivors of the Asian tsunami in 2005 and the relief effort in the US Gulf Coast for the communities stricken by Hurricane Katrina later that year. *Swift*'s speed and shallow draft meant that she could quickly carry relief supplies into ports rendered inaccessible to larger ships. It also marked the first ever helicopter embarkation and underway refuelling for *Swift* since her acceptance by the Navy in August 2003.

Swift proved she could not only get to trouble spots fast, she could operate with remarkable flexibility on a continuous basis. And, in 2006, she went on to support the fast evacuation of US citizens during the Lebanon emergency, followed by a general delivery of humanitarian aid to the Lebanese people. And both *Joint Venture* and *Spearhead* (the Army's HSV) have supported quick-response military operations in the Persian Gulf and other hotspots. *Joint Venture*, thanks to her speed, flexibility and shallow draft, was actually the most forward ship in the entire US Navy for the first few crucial hours of the Gulf War, acting as mother ship to Navy SEALs and Marine Corps teams seizing oil terminals at the entrance to the port of Umm.

Late in 2002, another good friend emerged in the guise of the Federal Trade Minister (and soon to be Deputy Prime Minister) Mark Vaile. Craig Clifford had formed a good working relationship with him during the ministry's residence on *Incat Tasmania* during the Olympics. Mark Vaile is a self-educated-through-TAFE realist with some sense of the real world. He was pivotal in obtaining a Federal Government surety for Incat from the government's Export Finance Insurance Corporation to the tune of A$52 million. This involved ABN AMRO Bank lending the money to pay off the National Australia Bank, but not yet the State of Tasmania. Once NAB got their pound of flesh, Incat had some money in hand to complete construction and delivery of hull 061 (*Swift*) for the US Navy. The State Government agreed to wait until the finished hull 058 was sold, which happened in May 2003; then the State of Tasmania got its money back, plus interest. Incat was finally free of debt.

The receivership was actually extinguished on Valentine's Day 2003, but the news from Mark Vaile came in the form of a Christmas present. Craig Clifford was engaged in the traditional manly pursuit of last-minute shopping on Christmas eve. Then the minister came on the phone just to clarify one or two details, as he put it, of the proposed deal, but the gist of the call was that Incat's long ordeal was over. It was the perfect present to take home to the family (Rebecca and a new-born) and a very nice piece of timing. As it happened, Craig Clifford's first son Joe had been born just a week after the arrival of the receivers; it had helped to keep things in perspective.

In fact, Incat actually started construction on no new vessels between June 2001 and December 2003, but the income from royalties on the military contracts kept the firm alive. As in aviation, the after-market and leasehold businesses had become significant contributors. After all, Incat had about 40 of the very big fast ferries at work all around the world by the end of 2008 and all of them continue to give service and to generate income. In fact, Incat has exported about 40 per cent of all the world's vehicle-carrying high speed ferries over 74 metres and 60 per cent of the world's high speed ferries with capacity of over 750 tonnes. (Remember, 60 per cent of all Rolls-Royce motor cars ever constructed are still in active service.) Just one Incat fast ferry has been mothballed—*Our Lady Patricia*—and she is serving as a spare-parts source for her sister ship on the Portsmouth to Ryde run after 25 years of loyal service. She, too, could have gone on indefinitely.

On 3 February 2003, Robert Clifford turned 60 (the age of 'retirement' in many places) just a few days before the receivership was finally discharged and control handed back to the directors. That was a nice birthday present. In theory, Incat and Clifford redeemed themselves and proved their point. In practice, Robert Clifford will look on the whole affair as unfinished business until the receiver finally pays back the A$2 million contingency fund held in reserve (another of those legal rules of receivership). It is difficult to calculate the actual costs of the receivership to Incat in money and reputational terms; possibly about A$20 million. But the firm saved a lot of money on salaries in the course of denting Robert Clifford's pride in his stewardship of the workers' welfare. He may have abused some of them from time to time but they were still, psychologically speaking, in his protectorate.

John Harris, the new managing director of the shipyard, announced the retirement of the receivers on Valentine's Day 2003 and made it clear Incat would be looking for an additional 80 workers immediately to work on hull 061 for the US Navy, with many more workers to follow. He also made it clear that the Incat operation in Hobart was essentially a 'factory' and that the company intended to fund any new developments from its own resources (to this day, Incat has steered clear of bank financing). Simultaneously, Craig Clifford moved across to run the increasingly-important charter business. His training as a lawyer made that a good fit.

Craig Clifford had foreseen Incat's central role in the industry back in 1999: 'We are now a shipbuilder, owner, financier and operator . . . all these roles are vital to establishing the market for fast ferries and establishing the industry standards. If we don't do it, who else would?'

So the new team was in place—Robert Clifford based in Woking as chairman and global super-salesman, John Harris as Managing Director of Incat Tasmania and the main manufacturing operations, Craig Clifford as MD of Incat Australia and Incat Chartering, Kim Clifford as MD of Incat Marketing, and Leith Thompson in Woking, Copenhagen and Hobart as MD Incat Finance and European Operations. A new chapter was about to start.

PART SIX

Onwards, ever upwards

The great quest resumes

49

'Movies are about their last twenty minutes'

At the time of writing, it is impossible to say what other rocks Robert Clifford may run his great enterprise onto. The biographer can only hint at the future. But there is no doubt that the receivership was the culminating, dramatic event in the ongoing saga—the turning point to triumph or disaster—twenty minutes before the end of the movie, according to Robert McKee's dictum.

In fact, the resolution of the receivership crisis was satisfyingly filmic—with Mark Vaile (the 'good' government minister), the Bollinger good guys and, of course, the loyal customers all riding over the hill as the US cavalry in the nick of time to rescue the company. So the hero was vindicated and the story turned out well. The receivers were defeated, although a proper cinematic denouement would require the bankers and the accountants to be humiliated and, preferably, wiped out. As it is, in the dull world of business reality, National Australia Bank and PricewaterhouseCoopers will merely move on to pastures new, occasionally pulling the plug on further small to medium-sized companies and adopting whatever new business model seems most likely to secure their wealth. And inventors and entrepreneurs like Robert Clifford will continue to struggle for financial support for their grand plans to do something useful in the real world of human affairs. It was ever thus.

On the surface, honours were about even after the event. The bank satisfied itself that it had no option but to instigate the receivership and Robert Clifford felt himself entirely vindicated by the way things turned out. And of course, from the entertainment point of view, the good folks of Hobart had the enjoyment of a long-running drama on their centre stage. It fell to Ray Pridmore (the bank's General Manager of Credit Restructuring) to play reluctantly the Jack Palance figure who is bested in the denouement of the movie. His reflection later was: 'I cannot stress strongly enough that there was absolutely no prospect of Incat ever trading out of the situation they were in without closing the business down. They had absolutely no money left and no means of securing any . . . I certainly believe that the Bank acted with the utmost patience and understanding throughout and has absolutely nothing with which to reproach itself.'

There is no reason to doubt a word of that, once you accept the rules and conventions of corporate financing—and once you accept the bank's gloomy opinion about the prospect of selling ships to the US military any time soon. The only other possible rescuer riding over the hill would have been the unlikely figure of John Howard, the Prime Minister, but once the February 2002 meeting with him and his ministers and advisers passed, the die was cast. From the point of view of the story, everything in the plotline hinged on the character of the hero, which is as it should be in a gripping story. Hardly anybody in Hobart was surprised by the receivership. They had seen the ships piling up in the bay and they knew that their favourite swashbuckler always sailed close to the wind. It's fair to say they were sad rather than surprised.

It's also fair to say that hardly anybody was surprised by the Houdini-like escape from the clutches of bankruptcy. That's what heroic figures are meant to do—escape in the nick of time. And nobody expected Robert Clifford to rein in his ambition as a consequence. Not so long after the receivership was extinguished, Incat began to build their biggest ever (112-metre) ferry in the new Wilson's shed. That's what the shed had been constructed for, so that's what came next (the bank, naturally, had disapproved of the decision to expand the production facility). *Incat the Magazine* of July 2003 (just five months after the end of the receivership) contained the gnomic announcement: 'We have commenced construction of our first 112 metre, but more of that later.' Once again, Clifford was back to his old 'bad habits' (as Ray Pridmore might see it) of building an entirely new kind of vessel 'on spec'. Well, not quite on spec because he was in deep negotiation over such a ship with one of the premier ferry operators in Japan, a relationship he had been nurturing for years. His nod in the direction of prudence was, this time, to begin building as usual—but *rather slowly*. So you might say he had been chastened by the receivership—but not much.

50

'Avid and sincere'

As it happens, the 'Letter of Intent' for the order of the first 112-metre vessel was not actually signed until 2006. Japanese businessmen do not move fast but they move exceeding surely. By the time you get into a contractual relationship, you can be confident there has been a long and steady relationship-building process at work, so that the contract is really no more than a formalisation of a much deeper understanding. This means that by the time you sign, you are likely to have become friends as well as business partners. And research indicates that business relations with Japanese firms are facilitated within more-or-less similar cultures.

As Robert Clifford points out, Tasmania is an island culture, historically dependent on its seaways and boat-builders for its sustenance. Yes, Japan is a bigger island culture (six times bigger by area) and there are more than 250 times as many occupants in its nearly 4000 islands, but the principle is the same—the character of the place is formed by the seaways. As it happens, Tasmania is just a bit smaller than Hokkaido, Japan's second island. And Hokkaido, in a sense mainland Japan's 'Tasmania', was the destination of the first 112-metre vessel sold to the Japanese. Hokkaido was the ancestral home of the very distinctive Ainu people, who spoke their own special language, subsisted partly on fishing, manufactured highly sophisticated craftworks and were reported to be especially hairy. It all sounds very Tasmanian.

More important still is the Japanese attitude to manufacturing integrity and excellence. The Japanese drive on the left-hand side of the road partly because their first railways systems were British-designed, but also because of the legacy of Clifford's hero Henry Royce—naturally, the early twentieth-century emperors had to be driven in a Rolls-Royce. Royce said: 'Strive for perfection in everything that you do. Take the best that exists and make it better. When it does not exist, design it!' That statement might have been the motto for Toyota or any of the other brilliant manufacturers that emerged from the rubble of the Second World War, and it had always inspired Robert Clifford. See the photograph in the illustrations of the two company chairmen—Yamamoto and Clifford. It is impossible not to see a shared reflection of the spirit of the Samurai.

That sense of friendship, mutual respect and shared values was palpable at the launching ceremony of the *Natchan Rera* in 2007. The Managing Director of Higashi Nihon Ferry described the vessel as his 'treasure ship' and went on to say: 'Several shipyards contacted us but we nominated Incat without any hesitation. It was because not only the state-of-the-art skills Incat possesses but also the passion of Chairman Clifford and all the Incat members towards the wave-piercing catamaran. We were, and still are, impressed by your avid and sincere attitude towards this project.' Avid and sincere captures it; you don't get that in a bog-standard business dedicated to making money. You are quite likely to get it in a firm created by an inventor dedicated to 'improving the breed' or changing the very character of a corner of the sea travel world.

When the orders finally came through from the US military, there was an immense amount of work to do on the new ships. Hull 061 (HSV-2 *Swift*) for the Navy had to be fitted out with all kinds of challenging new kit, including a helicopter deck with special night time and poor visibility lighting systems. Hull 061 had been just started when the financial crisis struck, so when the US Navy announced a 'short fuse open tender' for the new craft—which meant a very short delivery period—Incat was in a position to make and to deliver the new craft by August 2003. You could see this as a triumphant vindication of the Incat business model (being ready to move swiftly in the marketplace when necessary), or as yet another example of over-optimistic spec-building—take your pick. And the other military vessels—TSV-1X for the Army (which had been delivered in November 2002, in the middle of the receivership) and HSV-X1 *Joint Venture* (the multi-service platform for the Navy, Army, Marine Corps, Special Operations and Coast Guard)—were back for refit in 2004. The military tends to work these leased ships hard so the after-market for repair, refit and refurbishment represents a continuous work and income stream.

By 2004, the spread of the big Incat wave-piercers around the world was remarkable, considering that a smallish Hobart ship-builder had only been making such craft for 15 years. There were no fewer than six companies deploying the Incat boats in the English Channel (including such big names as P&O, Brittany Ferries, Condor Ferries and Hoverspeed) and another three on the Irish Sea (Sea Containers, Stena Line and the Isle of Man Steam Packet Company). Buquebus, SNAV and Transmediterranea were running the boats on the Mediterranean and Fred Olsen and Caribbean Ferries were out in the Atlantic Ocean. In the Americas, Bay Ferries and Buquebus were linking the United States to Canada and Argentina to Uruguay. And by the end of 2004, there were also companies running Incat fast ferries in the Far East, in the Baltic and in New Zealand. By the following year (2005), 83 per cent of all the high-speed vessels carrying passengers and vehicles around the United Kingdom had been built by Incat, and the number of big fast Incat ferries in operation all over the world had risen to 35.

51

Partners

Those fast ferries could not have been built and operated successfully without the creation of a whole series of partnerships
with Incat. The 'Tasmanian light shipbuilding cluster' illustrated
how many local supplier firms were dragged into world-class
performance by the insistent demands of Robert Clifford. But it
wasn't only the locals—major international engine manufacturers,
water-jet builders, seakeeping specialists, education institutions and
even classification societies all over the world were obliged to join
the game. Once he invented and built a new kind of ship, Robert
Clifford needed lighter and more powerful engines, more compact,
reliable and manoeuvrable water-jets, innovative means of ensuring
the comfort of passengers, a new breed of manufacturing workers
and an entirely fresh approach to certifying the safety of the vessels.

On the latter front, this meant an enduring partnership with
one of the world's great classification societies—Det Norske Veritas
(DNV)—established in Norway in 1864. You can't run a ship
without a licence, any more than you can take off in an aircraft
without very strict certification. So the classification societies are
the regulators and enforcers of quality and safety; and they are

strict. Except that in the case of Incat, there were no pre-existing standards for a very lightweight, fast, aluminium craft put together after the fashion of a very big aeroplane. So DNV and Incat had to work together to create the standards for a whole new class of vessel. DNV had the well-established reputation and the technical brainpower (more than 5000 specialist engineers worldwide) to work from first principles, rather than from a traditional 'cook book'. Tony Allwood, DNV's main man in Tasmania, points out: 'Certainly, Incat pushed DNV in some new directions that it might not otherwise have gone . . . in the past it was always DNV telling Incat to put some more metal here or there. Now it is quite often the case of Incat telling us that they are going to put more metal somewhere because it will make it a better ship.'

Another Scandinavian firm—the Finnish Wärtsilä—has supplied nearly all the powerful water-jets used by Incat ships. Established in 1834, Wärtsilä is typical of the naval engineering firms dotted around the Baltic and North Sea and in recent years the two firms have developed in lockstep. Incat obviously needed water-jet propulsion for high speed (the water-jet is no more than a very big pump that accelerates large quantities of water through a nozzle) and for manoeuvrability. As Incat moved into the military arena, it also had to be able to offer a very shallow draft for operations in non-standard (no docks) settings. Incat craft, thanks to the very compact and light LIPS water-jet system, can turn on a sixpence, manoeuvre sideways and come to a complete stop from 40 knots in just two and a half boat-lengths. Wärtsilä, which constructed and sold its first water-jet only in 1976, needed the stimulus of Incat's demands to develop its dominant position in the world water-jet marketplace. The maritime Tasmanian firm Incat gets on well with the Scandinavians, as with the seafaring Japanese. The Cliffords are meant to be English stock but look again at the cover photograph—most people see a Viking.

Perhaps the most important long-term partnership has been with the diesel engine-maker Ruston—latterly part of the German MAN

Group. Like Incat's partnerships in Scandinavia, the alliance with Ruston has a historical precedent. Ruston's predecessor originally made engines in Lincolnshire, beginning in 1840 (MAN also started its life in 1840 in Augsburg, Germany). They were building heavy oil engines in partnership with Hornsby of Grantham some years before the MAN Group (Maschinenfabrik Augsburg Nürnberg) gave Rudolf Diesel his chance to develop the first true diesel engines. Diesel was another of these characters (like Rolls and Clifford) given to experimenting dangerously with his inventions—he blew himself up and nearly died on the way to the first successful diesel prototype. MAN had produced the first ocean-going diesel marine engine in 1912. When the two firms, Ruston and MAN, finally came together in 2000 it looked like a long-delayed marriage made in heaven.

Of all Incat's collaborators, MAN/Ruston have been the most generous in acknowledging Incat's market-driven influence. They lead the world in marine diesels partly because of Robert Clifford's incessant prodding from the ship-building end. Not so different from Joseph Ruston who, back in 1857, bought into the Proctor & Burton company to form Ruston, Proctor & Company. He was a Clifford-like super-salesman of engines, focused entirely on the customers' problems. His motto was: 'My customer is my best friend.' He went to Russia in 1880 to sell pumping engines to drain the Pripet swamps, stopped off at the new oilfields in Baku on the way home to sell specialised oilfield engines, and eventually persuaded a group of Lancashire businessmen to build the Liverpool–Manchester Ship Canal—so he could sell them lots of mechanical excavators. He also invested in hugely expanded production facilities (to cope with optimistically anticipated demand) and deliberately built engines for stock—unheard of at the time—so he could serve the customer quickly. There is no record of problems with bankers but, anyway, he took the firm public in 1889, and there the similarity to Robert Clifford ends.

In a way, the sad side of the MAN/Ruston merger (sad for Britain anyway) is the transfer in 2005 of the making of the magnificent engines that power the big Incat ships from Newton-le-Willows near Manchester (the cradle of the railway revolution) to final assembly in Munich. The engines are tested in Saint-Nazaire in France and then shipped from Belgium to Hobart for installation by the same kinds of dedicated and ingenious craftsmen that Joseph Ruston used to employ all over the north of England. Manchester's loss is Munich's and Hobart's gain. So long as firms like Incat hold on to their manufacturing genius at home, Australia may cling to its making and doing bona fides. Once you dispense with manufacturing, you are at the mercy of international grazing and mining corporations and the dubious brilliance of the financial engineers.

In Part four, there is an account of Incat's partnership with Maritime Dynamics Industries—yet another example of Clifford's quest for perfection taking an entire industry forward into new territory. The T-foil stabilisation device, 'invented' on the back of a napkin in the Shipwright's Arms in Hobart, has become a standard piece of equipment in fast ferries all over the world—just as Robert Clifford's primitive scallop-tipper rewrote the rule-book for humble fishermen back in 1964. But, as with every technical innovation, there have been multiple modifications to the basic idea in practice. The Incat/Maritime Dynamics partnership continues to solve problems with T-foils in the endeavour to perfect their operation.

The basic T-foil device is a very effective way of creating computer-controlled lift in either direction in a fast ship so as to reduce vertical accelerations and hence seasickness. But the original foils (two not one) in *Condor 10* in 1992 worked very well indeed until sharp contact with a whale broke one of them and deposited a deal of blubber and stomach contents in the T-foil compartment. The next innovation was bolted-on foils designed to break when subjected to a certain load, and a dozen ships were so fitted. But foils continued to be lost because the world's oceans are full of debris and large mammals—so the latest centre-mounted foil is designed to retract in case of a strike. Nobody in the partnership thinks this is the last word on T-foils.

Almost from its inception, the College of Aluminium Training at the Incat shipyard (currently known as the Tasmanian Polytechnic/Tasmanian Skills Institute—Metal Trades) has likewise rewritten the international rule-book for training welders and others for the extraordinary demands of manufacturing an entirely new kind of ship. In 2008, the college was training a team of Thai trade teachers so they could upgrade skills in Thailand to support Incat operations in Asia. It is a good example of intelligent government infrastructural support because it quickly became the best facility of its kind in the world for producing truly skilled aluminium craftspeople.

The Incat partnership saga thus began with a group of on-site suppliers at Prince of Wales Bay—most of whom went on from servicing Incat to building international markets in fire protection, marine evacuation, cabin fitout and so on. But eventually, some of the biggest engineering firms in the world started to dance to the Incat tune. If you build a better mousetrap, the world will beat a path to your door. If you build a better ship (faster, more flexible and greener), you will have to make friends with international giants like Rio Tinto Alcan (for the improvement of aluminium alloys), MAN/Ruston, Wärtsilä, Det Norske Veritas and the rest). And all this happened because a butcher's son from Hobart, Tasmania, got the sailing bug when he was 13 years of age.

Then there are the competitors and rivals. If we accept the proposition that Robert Clifford is a major inventor of the twentieth century, then his invention of a particular kind of very fast seagoing craft created a raft of copy-cat rivals all around the world. That's how it goes in commercial competition. What made Clifford the inventor unusual was his refusal to bother with patent protection and his determination to share most of the company's intellectual property through the pages of *Incat the Magazine*. Effectively, he appointed himself leader and ambassador of the new global aluminium fast-ship industry, and became guarantor of standards of safety and quality in this newly emerging field. That was quite an assumption to make for an ex-fisherman. Taking on informal leadership of the industry certainly seemed to him to be a right—but, more than that, a duty.

Professor Michael Porter, the great guru of international competitiveness, drew attention to the curious interaction between fierce inter-company competition and enlightened industry and region collaboration—when the conditions are right (*The Competitive Advantage of Nations*, 1990). There is no love lost between Incat and the great local rival Austal, but it seems that both competition and higher order co-operation are necessary for the commercial uplift of entire industries, regions and nations. This seems to be what has happened in the world of the fast ferry—and Australia, unlikely as it may have seemed in the 1970s, has been a major beneficiary. So too has the environment: there is no doubt that these new kinds of ships, still evolving to take on bigger cargoes and wider roles, are part of the environmentally friendly solution when it comes to worldwide sea transport.

52

The green agenda

There are a great many ships in service all around the world and they exist in a bewildering variety. Since the first and most primitive craft constructed by our ancestors (a few of those vessels were catamarans), mankind has wanted and needed to travel across water, usually with some kind of cargo on board. A tiny proportion of large craft are powered today by wind and a very few (Robert Dane's Solar Sailor, see p. 145 and Robert Clifford's experimental wing, see p. 147) set out to harness the natural force of 'ground effect' wind or sunlight in combination with fuel-burning engines. But the vast majority of global shipping consists of very heavy steel vessels burning the cheapest fuel oil possible—the most polluting fossil fuel of all. Heavy oil comes in a number of forms, some of it barely distinguishable from road tar—which has to be heated even to flow—to lighter fuels which are still very impure. Heavy marine oils produce large quantities of sulphur dioxide, nitrogen oxide and other pollutants, and are thought to contribute around 9 per cent of all the world's air and sea pollution. They are insupportable in the future.

Incat has stuck with much more refined diesel fuels in all its ships. It is more expensive for the operator, but it will meet International

Maritime Organisation pollution guidelines into the future and, provided you consume it in a very efficient ship, it has advantages over the aviation quality kerosene burnt by gas turbine engines or compressed natural gas. Gas turbines have poor thermal efficiency and they are very expensive to run and maintain thus, as a general rule, only navies can afford them. Compressed natural gas might be a fuel of the future but there are problems of storage, range and safety. CODAG vessels (combined diesel and gas turbine) have their supporters but the complexity is daunting, especially as to the gearing of different engines to water-jets. As in every Incat vessel since 1990, the best solution is a compromise, but Robert Clifford knows that, as the ships get bigger, a time is likely to come when the advantages of the gas turbine may well prevail, particularly if very fast ferries (60 knots plus) make economic sense. But in the meantime, a 1000-passenger Incat vessel can travel 160 kilometres at 35 knots and burn less than 18 000 litres of fuel—that is just 0.18 litre per person per mile—cheaper than aircraft and most other mass transportation, and that's with the 500 tonnes of cars and cargo travelling free.

All of this thinking has been presented continuously in *Incat the Magazine* over the years. In it, Robert Clifford thinks out loud about the direction the industry is taking and pronounces on what ought to happen next. So, as ever, he tells the customers what is good for them and the authorities how they ought to order the worldwide industry. That may sound a bit bossy, but so far he has called most of the shots right. That is not to say he wins all the orders; when customers order an inferior (in his view) craft from a (in his view) substandard constructor, he can be as grumpy as the next proprietor. This is especially the case when a customer is (in his view) seduced by some fancy design or design feature which (in his view) won't work. The Clifford view is that the Incat-style lightweight catamaran with reserve buoyancy in the central hull is the right basic design for fast ships, because it obeys the laws of physics. This is the inventor speaking.

53

Physics and the purist

By asserting the iron laws of physics, Robert Clifford responds to a frequently-heard criticism of the Incat business model—that the company is a one-trick pony devoted to just one solution to complex challenges—and that it ought to 'diversify' so as to respond to a variety of markets. That was part of the criticism from the bank and from competitors when the receivership occurred—that Incat was over-reliant on one product. The truth is that Incat has always been remarkably responsive to customers' special requirements—fitting special ramps for the US Army, helicopter landing decks for the Navy, escalators and lifts for the Japanese, special ramps for on-board berths on the *Norman Arrow*, and reconfiguring ships for an enormous duty-free zone for Buquebus in South America. In the old days, a canny relationship manager in NAB understood the Incat business well. His replacements seem to have bought the conventional business school version of 'diversification'—based on very different kinds of markets and businesses.

Predictably, immediately after the receivership was extinguished in 2003, Robert Clifford mounted a doughty defence of the Incat business model. It amounted to a defence of Tom Peters' dictum in the famous book *In Search of Excellence* (1982)—'stick to your knitting' if you want to succeed in the long term:

> We have seen many shipyards divide their resources, attempting to be 'jack of all trades', build steel tugs, exotic plastic yachts, aluminium passenger ferries and composite patrol craft. We have seen most fail—it is, after all, very difficult to be good at everything. We at Incat do believe in diversity, but only within our sphere of expertise. Our Army, Navy and commercial 98 metre craft have all been tailored to suit their various missions. They are all quite different, yet based on a proven base technology. We do not build exotic composite mega-yachts for millionaires, as we do not have, or want to have, the skilled design engineers necessary to provide the special features of these craft, nor do we have the very specialised finishing skills required to satisfy the needs of very particular mega-yacht clients. We don't have the necessary skills and experience available to suit the design and construction of monohull naval patrol boats. To learn such skills would take many years of study.
>
> What we do have is very special and not to be wasted. We have special skills dedicated to extracting the maximum economy from an already proven product—a product that we have been perfecting for 20 years. The five 98m's built so far are developments of the six 96 metre, the four 91 metre and the four 86 metre craft. The 'devil is in the detail'—constant improvement has made the 98's by far the world's best fast ferries. A check will show our competitors don't even come close to matching our very impressive achievements.

This carefully-worded boast was accompanied by a chart demonstrating how the same power and fuel consumption (28 000 kW) uplifted nearly twice the tonnage in the 98-metre craft as compared with the 86-metre—truly a remarkable technological achievement. This is the statement of a purist who will not permit his enterprise to engage in pointless activity. What is made has to be made as perfectly as possible and be fit-for-purpose in some worthwhile endeavour. That means understanding and applying the physics. It is commerce allied to art/craft allied to science. It is unusual in the business world, and probably incomprehensible to most bankers.

Robert Clifford makes a similar assertion in relation to the best hull-form for fast sea transport. All ships sit on and pass through water; that is to state the obvious. But there are many ways of designing and moulding the hull or hulls. From the very first wave-piercers back in 1985–1986, the Incat team took their cue from nature; that is, from the laws of physics:

- Long skinny boats are always faster than fat ones.
- Wide ships always have the greatest stability and comfort.
- Low weight always requires less propulsive power.

That meant, right from the start, a catamaran made of aluminium riding on narrow floats.

All boat and ship design represents some kind of compromise or trade-off involving these variables. The familiar monohull is the simplest of all hull shapes and the easiest and cheapest to construct. No doubt the first boats of all were hollowed-out logs. Go to any rowing regatta and you will observe that all the shells look pretty much the same—long and skinny. But they have the luxury of progressing through smooth water. Bigger monohulls are often skinny and fast but they roll like the devil in rough seas and they have nothing like the carrying capacity and stability of a wide catamaran (compare the seakeeping of a fast warship with an expansive ocean liner).

Hydrofoils can go very fast because they effectively get the boat out of the frictional forces of water completely by riding on submerged wings. But they have to go fast because the lift/drag ratio is progressively degraded as the wings are asked to lift more weight and this restricts the potential payload—another trade-off. Hovercraft (technically 'surface effect ships') trade drag for wave-making by virtually eliminating friction. But the cost is the drag caused by the huge depression under the craft as it strives to stay 'afloat' on its very wide air cushion. Like the monohull, the hovercraft is not suited to bigger waves because of the loss of air pressure from under its skirt.

In recent years, some manufacturers have reverted to one of the oldest hull-forms of all—the trimaran—essentially a monohull with two outriggers for stability. Clifford likens it to a 'monohull with training wheels'. It represents an attempt to improve the carrying capacity of a long skinny monohull. But the outer hulls contribute little to the load-carrying ability, and they add weight and drag as they do their stabilising job. Furthermore, the trimaran does not lend itself to the practical realities of modern-day loading and unloading of big trucks. The simplest and quickest method (given that turnaround time is crucial for commercial ferry operation) is to drive a column of trucks onto the craft, swing around at the prow then come back ready for quick departure at destination. This transfer of 100 tonnes from one side to the other has no appreciable effect in a cat but causes a trimaran to heel over.

Robert Clifford is unusual in the fast ferry industry in having so much experience himself as an operator of ferries. This means he has always taken a keen interest (some would say in a bossy fashion) in his customers' operational problems: how to improve port facilities and turnaround times; judging the most efficient sailing speed for fuel economy; planning routes; managing crews cost-effectively, and so on. All of these considerations bear on the utility of any particular design: the cat solves or ameliorates most of them; the trimaran compounds them—for example, directional problems caused by the outriggers acting as rudders and in some conditions creating an unsettling flopping action from side to side. Also the tri has its main propulsion in the centre hull, so it requires a couple of expensive and heavy bow-thrusters for manoeuvring in port. The cat, with its simple and widely spaced rear water-jets, can turn on sixpence.

No design is perfect, all designs represent a compromise and physics is the great determinant. When Robert Clifford and Philip Hercus came up with the lightweight wave-piercing catamaran (with reserve lift and buoyancy held in the centre bow), they arrived at the least-worst way of propelling a ship quickly, comfortably and economically through a wide variety of water conditions. Until physics proffers a better way forward, the art consists in progressively improving the seakeeping and enlarging the size of this basically sound design. And the 'wing'—Robert Clifford's attempt to harness 'ground-effect' over water—may offer the next engagement with the basic physics of seafaring. The wing looks a bit more like an aircraft than a ship, but it does rely on three small hulls for support at rest—so not quite a trimaran.

54

Getting it right

Getting a design right is essentially a matter of the human comprehension of physics. Whoever first dreamed up the idea of a sail must have proceeded inductively from the experience of wind in the face allied to practical experiments with primitive bark 'boats'. The physics is a given; the trick for humankind is to apprehend the physics and then to invent something in alignment with nature. It requires a certain humility—something that sailors (despite drunken appearances) tend to possess, at least when they are ocean racing. At sea in a storm, nature calls the shots and survival is a great motivator and teacher. 'Getting it right' in ship design means understanding the physics of propulsion through a medium with the particular properties of water. You start with a 'feel' of things and progress to proper mathematics. Sailors really understand the meaning of the word 'risk'. Bankers imagine you can 'amortise' or 'collateralise' risk by using fancy maths—and we all know what happens when reality reasserts itself.

So way back in 1981, when Robert Clifford grasped that weight (and hence aluminium) would be the key to speed in the water, he and the naval architect Philip Hercus 'got it right' in the hull-form department as well. It had to be a cat—and Clifford figured out a way to construct the all-aluminium vessel quickly and cheaply. The same thing happened in 1985–1986 when they worked out that 'wave-piercing' represented the next incremental improvement (accommodation to nature) as the speeds increased. But they still needed to get the reserve buoyancy located in exactly the right place—dead centre for'ard—and the shape of the central hull exactly right for engagement with another of nature's little specialities—wave motions. Those experiments continue today.

You know you have got it right when you start to win races, or survive storms, or prove you can transport large numbers of people and matériel over the water much more safely and economically than other modes of transportation. The proof of the pudding is always in the eating. So physics is really very exciting in the context of discovery and challenge. Its apprehension supposedly lifted us, as a species, over all the other animals on the planet. Meccano seems to have disappeared from the playrooms or bedrooms of most homes these days—to be replaced by an insipid and pre-digested 'experience' cooked up by distant, pale-faced inventors of computer games.

Visit the Prince of Wales Bay shipyard in Hobart and you will find lots of happy and fulfilled people engaged in work that they love and that they know to be of real value in a world running out of oil. The work is intrinsically satisfying because you can see, however humble your role in the scheme of things, how your contribution adds to the magnificent whole—an object of beauty and evident usefulness. And they know that Incat makes a huge contribution to the wealth and well-being of the community they live in. And most important and impressive of all are the young apprentices learning the essential disciplines of physics in the real world. In those circumstances, under the watchful eye of Robert Clifford (Apprentice of the Year 1960) physics really is fun. Physics is the real thing.

That great Australian entrepreneur Dick Smith says Robert Clifford is a 'hero' of his for just this reason—he has always made useful products for use in the real world. Dick Smith's commercial achievements certainly match Robert Clifford's, but he remains in envy of the Clifford achievement because he (Smith) always really wanted to be a manufacturer. He actually started work after school in an electronics factory and got the bug there. So he sought out Robert Clifford many years later in an attempt to find out how on earth he did it—transformed himself from a school dunce and fisherman into the creator of one of the most complicated technology enterprises in the world. It is still a mystery to him—that leap from simple physics to high technology. How did he do it? Ask Clifford the same question and you get an incremental (*kaizen*) kind of answer. To the man himself it looks incremental rather than transformational or metamorphic. You build a good ship, you learn, you build a better ship, you learn, you build a much bigger ship, you learn some more . . . and so it goes on. Only to the outside observer does it seem to be a transformation. Smith calls it 'genius'.

It's no surprise that Dick Smith (a Clifford contemporary) was another Meccano addict. We really do need a serious retrospective study of the outstanding achievers of that generation, if only to ascertain the role of Meccano in that achievement. We might find a similar constellation of other factors too. Smith and Clifford share a startling number of formative influences typical for the time—hopeless at schoolwork, bullied for being different, dyslexic (at a time when nobody recognised the disadvantage), addicted to adventure, possessed of aspirational but not-very-rich parents and, perhaps crucially, subjected to the effects of a major business failure on the part of a father. Both of them were also exposed to a kind of 'value-adding throughput' process at a very young age: the four-year-old Clifford helping to supervise the manufacture of sausages; and the nearly as young Smith overseeing his mother's photographic retouching. We should never underestimate the power of observing a respected, older and wiser role model concentrating on making something useful happen in the real world. It doesn't happen much any more. It probably happened all the time in the family-business workshops of nineteenth century Clerkenwell, where William Clifford no doubt taught his sons something of the discipline and artistic eye needed to manufacture a thing of beauty. Maybe one of those sons carried the secret to Tasmania in 1889.

More to the point, both of them (Clifford and Smith) are men of honour. When their businesses got into trouble, they never contemplated the businessman's easy route to liquidation and a quick escape from creditors. They traded their way out of trouble. So they are mighty similar. But Dick Smith is no closer to an answer to the question: How did he do it? How did he get it so right?

55

Robert Clifford and 'marketing'

At the time of writing, Robert Clifford is still the main Incat salesman and inventor of market applications, and still doing it through a kind of enthusiastic partnership with those who buy and lease the ships. He turned 67 in February 2010 and shows few signs of slowing down. His father Fred survived till 89 years of age despite the debilitating kick in the chest by the racing trotter, and Eve Clifford, who died aged 96 early in 2010, was said right until the end of her life to be one of two or three women in the world who could order him about. The family say that the coming of grandchildren has mellowed him somewhat but the main task remains: to persuade the world that the aluminium wave-piercer is the correct answer to many of the world's shipping challenges. That is still the work-in-progress.

The standard business school take on a family-owned private firm like Incat involves terms like 'the succession' and 'managerial cadre' and 'exit strategy' and 'public flotation' and 'strategic alliance' (a euphemism for takeover by a major international corporation), but Incat remains a peculiarity in the business world. It is on a mission, and the mission has little to do with money-making or 'shareholder value' or market domination, and everything to do with fixing shipping. The main thrust is likely to remain the provision of bigger and better fast ferries. The dozen Incat ferries operating around the British Isles give sterling service to their operators and travellers, but they are increasingly the wrong size for modern demands—not big enough.

To prove that point, a brand new Incat 112-metre ship (hull 066) named *Norman Arrow* started a new Dover–Boulogne route in June 2009 and almost immediately transformed the character of the Channel crossing. Her high speed deadweight capacity is *five* times that of some of the earlier Incat fast ferries still operating on the English Channel and Irish Sea. The expanded shipyard at Prince of Wales Bay can easily accommodate much bigger vessels. The next step will be a 125-metre fast ferry offering 2000 tonnes deadweight (*twice* the capacity of the 112 metre at cruising speed).

The Dover–Boulogne ship shows the direction forward in a number of ways. Firstly, it was bought from Incat not by its operator, the French LD Lines, but by MGC Chartering, an Irish firm with over 25 years of expertise in aviation leasing. MGC have spotted an opportunity to transfer the aviation leasing model to shipping by buying up superior assets and leasing them to commercial and military operators all around the world. Secondly, at this sort of size, the main focus is on the carriage of cargo, not cars or people. To Robert Clifford's aesthetic relief, that means no heavy escalators or elevators as supplied in the Japanese 112-metre vessel. Even the drive shafts of the new ship are now made of carbon-fibre to save weight.

If cargo is the main game, the carriage of all kinds of vehicles and their occupants represents a kind of profitable bonus. Darryl Tishler, MGC Chartering's Director, says:

In choosing the Incat 112 metre we have drawn lessons from the aviation model, for example the ever-increasing importance of minimising fuel burn and environmental impact. The . . .

112 metre is built to be as light as possible. It consumes clean diesel (and) for maximum efficiency it offers dual-speed operation (23 or 40 knots). NOx emissions are less than 10g/kWh and importantly it burns less fuel per cargo tonne per nautical mile than any other high speed ferry built to date. The economic and environmental credentials of the Incat 112 metre wave-piercing catamaran are outstanding.

Mr Tishler, a customer, is restating the 'if you build a better mousetrap . . .' dictum. Robert Clifford, as 'marketer', never targeted the aviation leasing market or the carriage of cargo. Nor did he originally envisage military applications for the ships Incat was designing and improving. The quest was always to build a better ship. If you build a better ship—lighter, faster, more flexible, more environmentally friendly—the applications will follow. LD Lines are mainly interested in cargo and therefore in even larger fast ships.

These new developments throw some light on the field generally described as marketing in the business school world. The word 'marketing' appeared on the scene in the earlier part of the twentieth century at just the moment in history when most Americans found they had more money than they knew what do with. The big corporations knew what they should do with it—spend it on increasingly unnecessary wants dressed up as 'needs'. Alfred P. Sloan, the long-time president and chairman of General Motors, managed to sell pretty much the same motor car under a bewildering array of different 'brands'—each carefully targeted at particular demographic segments of aspirational Americans. As the world starts to run out of natural resources and to worry about despoliation of the environment, it looks very much as though the rich nations are beginning to adjust to purchasing based on actual need rather than the wants provoked by the 'marketing profession'.

The peculiarity of Robert Clifford and Incat, throughout their 25 years of serious ship-building, is that they have never really contorted themselves so as to do exactly what their 'market' wants.

Indeed, Clifford has been forthright in consistently offering to the customers what he believes they really need and entering into vigorous discussion about any adaptations required. This is not what you are told to do by the marketing textbooks; the idea is to assume the customer really is 'always right', even if you think you know better. It was like this over bow doors and over the carriage of heavy trucks. Robert Clifford took a view on what the customers' situation required and provided accordingly. As he pointed out: 'I know we lost sales to Austal because they were willing to give the customer a ship with a bow door . . . we can almost always convince the customers that it is in their best interests but there are occasions when they just don't understand their own business!' This assertion represents, to say the least, a novel approach to marketing. It is certainly not what the business schools teach.

At the time of writing, Austal, the great Australian competitor, has a 127-metre trimaran design for a new 'littoral combat ship' in sea trials for the US Navy—a fantastic achievement for a young Australian company. That is a competition that Austal won against the old enemy (Incat), but in Austal's case working in harness with the enormous General Dynamics Corporation on a ship built in Mobile, Alabama. It's safe to say that the LCS *Independence* (an entirely new design concept worked out exactly for the Navy specification) is a good example of textbook marketing, providing a very rich customer with exactly what he asks for—in this case a very expensive innovation. The Incat alternative was, of course, a modification of the tried-and-tested wave-piercer. You can't win them all.

So Robert Clifford is, and always was, 'market oriented'. It's just that his view of the fast ship market always was that it is still developing fast and that Incat can afford to be at the leading edge of market developments, even if that means losing a sale or two because some customers don't share that vision—yet. That is the yachtsperson's instinct—get into the lead and stay ahead by artful tacking in the fluky winds. Way back in the late 1950s, he had grasped the yachting principle: 'There is no such thing as a postponed decision because in 10 minutes' time it's a different decision!' It is also a view of marketing that you can impose upon a company if you happen to own most of it. Business schools these days draw attention to the important distinction between an *output* (what you sell to the customer) and an *outcome* (the value added by the customer once he has your product in use). Right from the start, Incat 'marketed' outcomes.

This view of marketing is reminiscent of the automobile industry in the post-war years. The British industry slowly lost its ascendancy because the cars it manufactured became less and less reliable in use. But the marketing was absolutely brilliant—it has to be if the customer is to be persuaded to buy a good-looking but mechanically substandard product. Meanwhile, Mercedes were methodically crash-testing hundreds of cars in order to improve survivability for passengers, and Toyota were learning from W. Edwards Deming how to build a virtually flaw-free vehicle. It's not that Mercedes and Toyota were unmindful of marketing; it's just that the engineers held some sway in the boardroom. British car manufacturing was in the iron grip of the money men looking to boost the share price in the short term. The Germans and Japanese knew they were in the automotive business and that the money was an agreeable by-product. The British car-makers were essentially in the money business, but they were stuck with the need to build these pesky motor car things. Paying attention to the intrinsic properties of the product pays off in the end. As if to prove the point, Toyota only got into big trouble in 2009 after they took their eye off the technical ball and decided to go hell-for-leather for market share. Their aim became, as the Toyota chairman confessed, to overtake General Motors as the biggest car manufacturer in the world.

Far from being inflexible, Incat is not even above offering a variant of the wave-piercer for super-rich clients in search of a 'super yacht tender' designed to cart their various luxury boats and helicopters around to the world's fleshpots. The range of tasks the basic ship can perform is wide indeed. There is no doubt that the military will be back, because the Incat offering is so attractive in terms of speed, payload, versatility, reliability and cost—and the basic platform is so adaptable. A betting man would place a few dollars on the wing as the next great product breakthrough.

56

The role model

Most proper businessmen (of the kind that banks are comfortable with) start to contemplate their retirement pension-pots when they get into their fifties. Nobody ever thought that Robert Clifford was that kind of businessman. This biographer decided early on that Clifford is a businessman only because getting into business was the requirement for pursuing his creative life's work. That work consists in inventing, making and doing in the context of water. He does share an intense competitiveness with most businesspeople, so he dislikes losing a contest just as much now as he did when sailing in competition on the Derwent as a teenager. But in sports, as in business, there are always two aspects to the game—mastery of technique and winning. Too many business and sports people are obsessed with winning at any cost. Robert Clifford loves to win, but he is also engaged in a higher order contest with the elements and with physics. In the long run, that is what turns him on.

It is this purist (some might say obsessional) aspect of Robert Clifford that makes him the ideal role model for all those young Australians wired-up mainly for working with materials to make things. Observe any infant playgroup and you will see how natural, stimulating, and educative it is for very young people to grapple with apprehending, shaping and making. It is truly one of the joys of life, and it remains so for those fortunate adults not entirely seduced by book-learning and abstraction. But there is more to it than that—every country needs its engineers and manufacturers and, we are told, most countries (with the exception possibly of China) now face a drought of able young entrants to the making-and-doing trades and professions. There is no shortage, however, of aspirant spin-doctors, bankers, lawyers and management consultants. An early trip on an Incat ferry might be enough to turn on a bright and enterprising youngster, but there is no harm in also having to hand an account of the life of this unlikely hero.

What happens to the great man next? Well, nobody expected creatives like Otto Klemperer or Pablo Picasso to 'retire' when they got to 65; they were just beginning to get the hang of their life's work. They both made lots of money but that wasn't the purpose of the work. Klemperer conducted his last concert at 87 (your biographer was there), and Picasso did his last sketch at 90. There is an apocryphal story that his doctor showed Picasso the X-ray of what ailed him on his deathbed. Picasso is supposed to have grabbed it and started to scrawl interesting shapes and compositions on it. Then he died, still improving the work . . .

Bibliography

Bateson, Gregory. *Mind and Nature: A Necessary Unity*, Dutton, New York, 1979.

Bion, Wilfred. R. 'On Arrogance', *International Journal of Psychoanalysis*, vol. 39, 1958, pp. 144–6.

Buffett, Warren F. *Annual Letter to Shareholders*, Berkshire Hathaway Inc., www.berkshire-hathaway.com, 2003.

Gardner, Howard. *Frames of Mind: The Theory of Multiple Intelligences*, Basic Books, New York, 1983.

——*Leading Minds: An Anatomy of Leadership*, Harper Collins, London, 1996.

Golding, William. *Rites of Passage*. Faber & Faber, London, 1980.

Hampden-Turner, Charles et al. *The Seven Cultures of Capitalism*, Currency Doubleday, New York, 1993.

Harvey-Jones, John. *Getting it Together: Memoirs of a Troubleshooter*, Heinemann, London, 1991.

Hilsman, Robert. *To Move a Nation*, New York, Doubleday, 1967, quoted in P. Watzlawick et al. *Change: Principles of Problem Formulation and Problem Resolution*, Norton, New York, 1974.

Hudson, Liam. 'Fertility in the Arts and Sciences', *Social Studies of Science*, vol. 3, 1973, pp. 305–10.

Incat the Magazine, vol. 3, no. 16, 2002.

Jacobsen, Mary-Elaine. *The Gifted Adult*, Ballantine Books, New York, 2000.

Kroto, Sir Harry. 'The Meccano Man', interviewed by Shirley Dent, *New Humanist*, vol. 117, issue 1, Spring 2002.

Li, Jiatao. *Managing International Ventures in China*, Pergamon, Oxford, 2001.

Mant, Alistair. *Intelligent Leadership*, Allen & Unwin, Sydney, 1997.

McGaughey, Sara L. et al. 'An Unconventional Approach to Intellectual Property Protection: The Case of an Australian Firm Transferring Shipbuilding Technologies to China', *Journal of World Business*, vol. 35, issue 1, Spring 2000, pp. 1–20.

McKee, Robert. *Story: Substance, Structure, Style and the Principles of Screenwriting*, Methuen, London, 1999.

Peters, Tom et al. *In Search of Excellence*, Grand Central Publishing, New York, 1982.

Porter, Michael E. *The Competitive Advantage of Nations*, Macmillan, London, 1990.

Ruthven, Phil. *Leadership and Success in Corporate Australia*, IBIS Business Papers, IBIS, Melbourne, 1994.

Stamp, Gillian. *Brief Notes on Capability*, BIOSS paper, 1988.

Suskind, Ron. *The Price of Loyalty: George W. Bush, the White House, and the Education of Paul O'Neill*, Simon & Schuster, New York, 2004.

Wickham, Mark D. 'Reconceptualising Porter's Diamond for the Australian Context', *Journal of New Business Ideas and Trends*, vol. 3, issue 2, 2005, pp. 40–8.

Index

Index

Index

Index